TRANSPORT RESEARCH LABORATORY
Department of Transport

STATE-OF-THE-ART REVIEW  8

# FATIGUE OF STEEL BRIDGE DECKS

## by Tim Gurney

London:  HMSO

HMSO publications are available from:

**HMSO Publications Centre**
(Mail, fax and telephone orders only)
PO Box 276, London, SW8 5DT
Telephone orders 071-873 9090
General enquiries 071-873 0011
(queuing system in operation for both numbers)
Fax orders 071-873 8200

**HMSO Bookshops**
49 High Holborn, London, WC1V 6HB
(counter service only)
071-873 0011 Fax 071-873 8200
258 Broad Street, Birmingham, B1 2HE
021-643 3740 Fax 021-643 6510
Southey House, 33 Wine Street, Bristol, BS1 2BQ
0272 264306 Fax 0272 294515
9-21 Princess Street, Manchester, M60 8AS
061-834 7201 Fax 061-833 0634
16 Arthur Street, Belfast, BT1 4GD
0232 238451 Fax 0232 235401
71 Lothian Road, Edinburgh, EH3 9AZ
031-228 4181 Fax 031-229 2734

**HMSO's Accredited Agents**
(see Yellow Pages)

*and through good booksellers*

# Contents

# Foreword

This review describes work for the Department of Transport managed by TRRL and carried out between 1963 and 1987. Throughout this period the research was led by Dudley Nunn and it was through his technical competence and foresight that so much was accomplished at a time when there was no comparable work elsewhere.

At the time the work started steel bridges were being designed to BS 153, 'Specification for steel girder bridges', which had been first published in 1923 and successively revised in 1933, 1958 and later in 1972. In the 1960s fatigue was known to designers but considered to be unlikely to occur in practice. It was as a result of the recommendations of RRL's Research Advisory Committee, chaired by the late Dr Kerensky, that it was decided to commence research on a number of topics including traffic usage, surfacings and fatigue of steel highway bridges. A broadly based investigation was set up and in 1966, using laboratory data along with a best estimate of traffic loading, Nunn predicted that fatigue cracking could occur within the assessed design life of an orthotropic steel deck. In 1968 cracks developed in the trough stiffener to cross-beam welds of an orthotropic panel installed as part of the TRRL experimental programme in the A40 at Denham, after some 4$^1$/$_2$ years' trafficking. In 1971 cracks were found in the welded connections between temporary flotation diaphragms and the trough stiffeners of the deck of the Severn Bridge, after 5 years' trafficking. In the time since then fatigue cracks have occurred in orthotropic decks all over the world and Nunn's predictions were fully confirmed. Maintenance Authorities and designers have now become aware of the problem and design of orthotropic decks is recognised as being dominated by fatigue considerations.

The TRRL investigation fell into two phases; between 1963 and 1972 when the work was mainly predictive and between 1972 and 1987 when methods of assessment and repair were investigated. Some of the early results were used in support of the new design standard BS 5400 'Steel, concrete and composite bridges' Part 10 'Code of practice for fatigue' published in 1980.

Much of the work was carried out by TRRL staff in the laboratory at Crowthorne, at the Denham test site, and on bridges in the field. In addition, a very significant contribution was made throughout the investigation by the author of this review, Dr Gurney of the Welding Institute, and by other contractors to TRRL.

The work has been recorded in internal notes at TRRL and reports by contractors but much of it has not been generally available until publication of this review. A number of major steel bridges are now coming to an age when it is prudent for Maintenance Authorities to assess the likelihood of fatigue cracking. Moreover there are several new steel bridges under construction or being designed which can profit from the past experience. It is therefore timely to publish the experimental data and analyses of the 24 years' work on fatigue of steel bridge decks in the laboratory and field. Hopefully it will be of interest to designers, maintenance engineers and researchers.

Dr G P Tilly

# 1  INTRODUCTION

In order to achieve economy in the design of steel bridges one of the main aims must inevitably be to reduce to a minimum the dead weight of the superstructure, and this is particularly so in the case of long span and lifting bridges. One way to assist in the achievement of that objective is, of course, to avoid the use of heavy bridge decks.

Although there is more than one possible approach to that problem, a fairly obvious one is to make use of a welded steel deck plate, since that eliminates the relatively heavy concrete deck which is an inevitable feature of composite construction. Typically a concrete deck might be expected to weigh about four times as much as an orthotropic steel deck.

The orthotropic deck consists of a deck plate supported in two mutually perpendicular directions by a system of transverse 'crossbeams' and longitudinal stiffeners. It may therefore be likened to a plate with dissimilar elastic properties in the two directions; in other words it is effectively an ORTHOgonal anisoTROPIC plate or, for brevity, an 'orthotropic plate'. In this form of construction the deck itself can form the top flange of the main load-carrying member making up the bridge; in some instances it has, for example, formed the top flange of a box girder.

The basic layout of an orthotropic bridge deck is shown in Fig. 1.1. The most notable variant is the form of the longitudinal stiffeners which may be either open ribs, such as flat bars, angles or bulb sections, or closed sections (usually of trapezoidal, V or rounded section). Clearly the latter are much stiffer in torsion.

In a sense the orthotropic deck was a development of the 'battledeck' floor of the 1930s. That consisted (see Fig. 1.2) of a steel deck plate welded to longitudinal (normally I-beam) stringers, which were supported by cross girders. It will be noted that, in that system, the deck plate played no part in strengthening the cross girders or forming part of their top flanges; nor did it contribute to the strength of the main longitudinal girders. It was merely there to transmit the wheel loads transversely into the stringers.

Clearly the battledeck was not the most efficient possible system, but it did provide evidence that the strength of a flat steel plate subjected to localised wheel loads was considerably higher than had been anticipated; hence the birth of the orthotropic deck.

Originally, the main stimulus for the development of orthotropic decks came from the need to rebuild various long-span bridges in Germany after World War II, against a background of steel being in short supply. As far as is known, the first such bridge was the Kurpfalz bridge over the River Neckar in Mannheim (1950), while the first suspension bridge to have an orthotropic deck was the Cologne-Muelheim Bridge over the Rhine, completed in 1951. Both these bridges had open rib longitudinal stiffeners; the use of torsionally stiff closed ribs came a few years later. Further impetus to the use of orthotropic decks was provided by their relatively low weight, which made them attractive where a high degree of pre-fabrication or rapid erection was required.

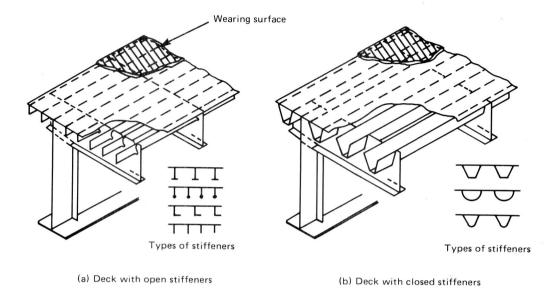

Figure 1.1 Two basic types of orthotropic steel bridge decks

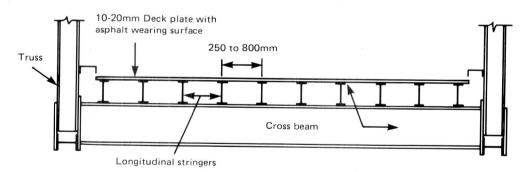

Figure 1.2 Typical cross-section of bridge with 'battledeck' floor

In addition the development of weldable high strength steels enabled further desirable reductions in deck weight to be obtained.

As far as Britain is concerned the first two major bridges to have orthotropic decks, both designed by Freeman Fox and Partners, were the Forth road bridge, opened in 1964, and the Severn crossing, opened in 1966. The latter consists essentially of three adjacent structures, the Severn bridge, Beachley Viaduct and the Wye bridge, but all have the same design of orthotropic steel deck. More recently there have been several others, such as Avonmouth (1974), Erskine (1971), Kessock (1982) and Humber (1981), to name a random selection.

2

Even though relatively few in number, these long span road bridges almost inevitably form strategically important road links and represent major capital investments. By way of example, the Severn Crossing carries about two million heavy goods vehicles per year between England and Wales and cost about £11 million to build in 1966; the second Severn Crossing, due to be constructed in the fairly near future, is expected to cost about £150 million, plus another £100 million for the approach roads.

## 1.1 Summary of the British work

The research which has been carried out on orthotropic decks in Britain originated from the use, or proposed use, of such decks on the Forth and Severn bridges. While both were built to British Standard BS 153, which was current at the time, that was a Standard for 'Steel Girder Bridges' and the fatigue clauses made no special allowance for the complexities of orthotropic decks. Indeed, by today's standards, the fatigue clauses were rather rudimentary. Yet it was obvious that some of the details involved in the design of the decks were potentially liable to cause fatigue problems and it was felt desirable to investigate whether or not those fears were well founded. A summary of the main joints which were considered to be 'at risk', and for which few, if any, experimental fatigue test results existed at the time, is shown in Fig. 1.3.

The first exercise represented an attempt to measure, experimentally, the stresses which might occur in an orthotropic deck under traffic loading. To this end two sections of deck, similar to those which were intended to be used for the Severn bridge, were built into the London to

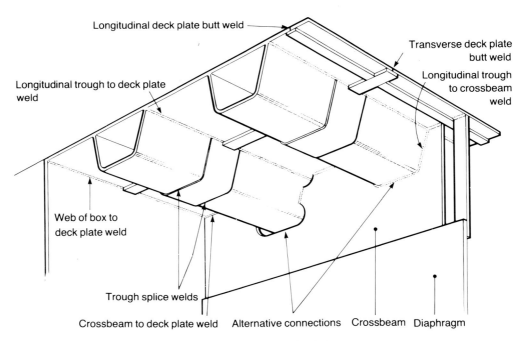

Longitudinal deck plate butt weld

Transverse deck plate butt weld

Longitudinal trough to crossbeam weld

Longitudinal trough to deck plate weld

Web of box to deck plate weld

Trough splice welds

Crossbeam to deck plate weld · Alternative connections · Crossbeam · Diaphragm

*Figure 1.3    Main welded connections in a typical orthotropic bridge deck*

3

Fishguard trunk road (A40) at Denham in 1963. They were positioned over a pit which allowed access to the underside of the deck for inspection, the installation of strain gauges, etc. At the same time the experiment was intended to incorporate a trial of various possible surfacings, namely two 1 1/2 inch (38mm) thick asphalts and four different resin based surfacings each 3/8 inch (10mm) thick.

While there is some doubt as to whether the deck used in this experiment was fabricated in precisely the same way as the actual bridge deck, and while it is certain that conditions at the Denham test site and at the bridge were not identical (for example there were virtually no dead load or wind load stresses at the Denham site), it was interesting to find that after about 4 1/2 years fatigue cracks developed in some of the trough to cross-beam welds. All of these cracks were located in the panel with the epoxy resin surfacing. This effectively confirmed that there was at least a need to examine the fatigue problem in rather more detail.

More recently that need has been confirmed in a very direct way, since fatigue cracking has been reported in several bridge decks in many different countries. Among others it certainly exists, for example, in France, Germany, Holland and UK and has been found in most of the details outlined in Fig. 1.3.

In essence, fatigue assessment requires knowledge of:

a)      the loading spectrum;
b)      the corresponding stress spectra for each joint under consideration;
c)      the relevant constant amplitude S-N curve for that joint.

In the course of the work reviewed in this document each of these aspects of the problem has been studied, but with emphasis on the last two.

As far as the derivation of stress spectra is concerned, the approach mainly involved strain measurements at standard distances from each type of joint, both in the laboratory and on site. In the laboratory the work involved the derivation of stress influence lines for a single static wheel applied to a full-scale model deck; typically this necessitated taking measurements with the wheel and axle assembly positioned at some 900 different locations.

Influence lines for the 'mix' of heavy goods vehicles (HGV) defined in the UK Bridge Design Code, BS 5400 (Part 10, Table 11), were then calculated by superposition of the relevant single wheel stresses, and the rainflow cycle counting method was used to derive the stress spectrum for each gauge position.

Influence lines were also obtained from load tests on existing bridges, using a standard test vehicle. In many instances the influence lines were so short that it was again possible to derive the stresses for a single wheel.

A third method of obtaining stress data was to monitor stresses at welded joints on a bridge under normal traffic. This enabled the stress spectrum for each joint to be recorded and used to estimate fatigue life without many of the assumptions inherent in the other methods.

In the course of the work it was found that the surfacing can have a profound effect upon the stresses in some of the joints and a considerable amount of work was carried out to try to define the influence of the surfacing. Unfortunately it was found that the stress reduction caused by the surfacing, although it could be large, was very variable and difficult to quantify. For example, it was found to depend upon the material properties of the surfacing, the ability of the waterproofing layer to transmit shear stress between the surfacing and the steel deck plate, and the distance of the particular welded joint from the deck plate. While the latter two variables can be allowed for relatively easily, it is difficult to allow for the material properties since the stiffness of asphalt (and hence its ability to reduce stress in the deck) varies both with temperature and with rate of loading in a non-linear manner; for example surfacing is stiffer at high rates of loading (i.e. under free flowing traffic). Another problem is that composite action can be reduced if the surfacing cracks over hard spots in the deck, such as a longitudinal web.

With regard to the definition of the basic S-N curves for the various types of joint, it is first necessary to recognise that the reason why the fatigue design of steel decks was specifically omitted from BS 5400 was that the S-N curves in that Standard were known not to be applicable. By their nature joints in orthotropic decks are subjected to complex stress distributions with high stress gradients around the joints and there is evidence that the fatigue strength of thin plates in bending, as is often the situation in orthotropic decks, is different from thicker plates under axial loading.

Constant amplitude fatigue tests have therefore been carried out on most of the types of joints that may exist in a typical orthotropic deck. Specifically, results have been obtained for:

1)      trough to cross-beam joints
2)      trough to deck joints
3)      trough splices
4)      butt joints in the deck
5)      cross-beam to deck joints (but the results were also assumed to be applicable to longitudinal web to deck joints).

In addition, in the light of actual or anticipated fatigue cracking in service, repair and strengthening methods have been investigated for several of these joints; they are considered in conjunction with the basic fatigue results for the relevant type of joint.

Over the years there have been significant changes in the detail design of orthotropic decks. For example, in the Severn, Forth and Wye bridges, built in the 1960s, the longitudinal deck stiffeners were trapezoidal in shape and about 3-4$^{1}/_{2}$ metres long; they were butted up to the transverse cross-beams and fillet welded all round. Subsequently, in bridges built in the UK after about 1970, V shaped longitudinal stiffeners about 14m long were used. These passed through cut-outs in the cross-beams and the V-stiffeners themselves were joined end to end some distance away from the cross-beams. In the course of the work tests have been carried out on both types of design.

Finally, as a result of the information derived in the experimental work outlined above, a substantial amount of work was put into using the data to predict fatigue lives.

## 1.2　The Denham experiments

As indicated previously, the first fatigue cracks to occur in an orthotropic deck in this country were those in the experimental deck which was built into the A40 trunk road at Denham in 1963. Although not of major significance now, in the light of all the work which followed, no review of British work would be complete without some reference to those experiments.

As was also noted in the Introduction, the use of orthotropic decks stems largely from a need to reduce, as far as possible, the dead weight of the superstructure. Thus, knowing that such decks were to be used on the Forth and Severn Bridges, it was recognised (in the mid 1960s) that the low deck weight might have the effect of increasing the live (traffic) load stresses in the deck to such an extent that they would be in the 'fatigue range'. It was therefore felt necessary to measure the stresses which actually occurred in a typical deck under real traffic loading. At the same time it was decided to combine the experiment with comparative trials of various resin-based and asphalt surfacings, which had been intended to take place elsewhere.

To this end two deck panels to the same design as those which were intended to be used on the Severn Bridge, were installed in the nearside (slow) lane of the carriageway. They were placed over a concrete pit which had the functions of (a) supporting the deck panels in a manner similar to a bridge structure, and (b) allowing access to the underside of the panels to permit the wiring-up of strain gauges and the installation of transducers, etc. Nevertheless there were some differences between the support conditions for the test panels and for the actual bridges. The site was also equipped with a dynamic weighbridge and a pneumatic tube axle counter.

The size of the test panel was dictated by the requirement that the local stresses and deformations under wheel loading should be comparable with those in larger panels forming the carriageway of a bridge (i.e. 24 ft wide for a two-lane road). The width of the panels was fixed from a consideration of the probable width of the wheel tracks of the nearside wheels of vehicles passing over the site. It was estimated that the tracks of the nearside wheels would be concentrated in a lane 4 ft wide and that a margin of 4 ft should be allowed on either side of this lane to reduce edge effects. The width of the panels as constructed was 13 ft. The length of the plates was a compromise between the wish to test as many different types of surfacing material as possible and the cost of fabricating and installing large panels. Each panel was 52 ft long, and comprised two central sections with 15 ft spacing between transverse stiffeners, and two 11 ft long end sections. The reduced length of the end sections was intended to compensate for the loss of the additional stiffness that would exist if the plate were continued over the end cross-girders. Details of the panels are shown in Fig. 1.4. One of them was surfaced with 4 different 9mm thick resin-based materials and the other with two 38mm thick asphalts. The difference in the thickness of the surfacings was allowed for by an increase in the height of the supporting walls under the former panel.

The test site was constructed in the autumn of 1963 and opened to traffic on 27 November 1963. It was finally closed in January 1973 owing to reconstruction of the carriageway.

As far as fatigue cracking is concerned, it was found in March 1968 that three of the longitudinal stiffener to cross-beam welds on the panel with resin surfacings had cracked through the weld throat. The welds affected were on the stiffener located under the maximum of the wheel track

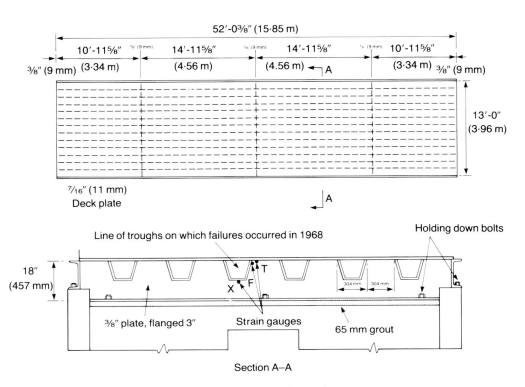

**52'-0⅜" (15·85 m)**

| 10'-11⅝" | ⅜" (9 mm) | 14'-11⅝" | ⅜" (9 mm) | 14'-11⅝" | ⅜" (9 mm) | 10'-11⅝" |
|---|---|---|---|---|---|---|
| ⅜" (9 mm) (3·34 m) | | (4·56 m) | | (4·56 m) ←A | | (3·34 m) ⅜" (9 mm) |

**13'-0" (3·96 m)**

⁷⁄₁₆" (11 mm)
Deck plate

A

Line of troughs on which failures occurred in 1968

Holding down bolts

18"
(457 mm)

T
X F

304 mm  304 mm

⅜" plate, flanged 3"       Strain gauges       65 mm grout

Section A–A

*Figure 1.4   Details of the experimental panels installed in the A40 at Denham*

distribution curve. Subsequently, by the time that the panel was finally removed in 1973, further cracking occurred in similar positions on that panel. However, no failures were detected in the panel with asphalt surfacing except in one case, where it was found that a lack of side-wall fusion defect had extended by fatigue.

At the time there was, initially, some surprise that fatigue cracking should have occurred in that particular joint, since it was nominally in compression and the panels were fabricated under longitudinal pressure, in the hope that there would be contact between the stiffeners and the cross-beam. In reality, however, when cracking occurred there was a gap, at least in one case, of up to 1mm between the weld and the cross-beam indicating that, at failure, the stiffener pulled away from the cross-beam. After this cracking had occurred there was noticeable closing of the gap when heavy vehicles passed over the panel.

In effect it was this experience at Denham which set the scene for an investigation which was to continue for many years and which this book attempts to summarise.

# 2 TRAFFIC LOADING

As was noted in Chapter 1, knowledge of the expected traffic loading is an obvious essential pre-requisite for the adequate fatigue design of an orthotropic deck, or indeed of any other highway structure. However, with an orthotropic deck the problem is more complicated than simply requiring a knowledge of the total traffic flow. Since fatigue cracking, if it occurs, is essentially caused by local loading conditions, there is certainly a need to know the distribution of loading between traffic lanes and indeed the lateral distribution of wheel loads within a lane. In addition, since the stiffening effect of the surfacing is dependent upon temperature, it is necessary to know the likely distribution of traffic flow over the year and also through the day.

## 2.1 Overall traffic flow

In Britain, the fatigue design of highway bridges is normally based upon the Standard Load Spectrum and information on the number of commercial vehicles per lane per year, both of which are defined in BS 5400, Part 10. The Standard Load Spectrum is as shown in Table 2.1, while the annual flow of commercial vehicles on major roads is assumed to be as shown in Table 2.2. It will be noted that, in addition to the 'Construction and Use' vehicles (i.e. those allowed to travel freely) defined in Table 2.1, there are 500 'special' (i.e. larger) vehicles per million (i.e. those which require special permits), but their contribution to fatigue damage in bridge decks is

**TABLE 2.1    STANDARD LOAD SPECTRUM FOR 'CONSTRUCTION AND USE' VEHICLES.**

| Vehicle type | Loading group | Axle loads (kN) | | | | | No in each group per million HGVs |
|---|---|---|---|---|---|---|---|
| 5 axle articulated | medium | 60 | 70 | 70 | 80 | 80 | 14500 |
| | low | 40 | 45 | 45 | 60 | 60 | 15000 |
| 4 axle articulated | high | | 55 | 100 | 90 | 90 | 90000 |
| | medium | | 45 | 85 | 65 | 65 | 90000 |
| | low | | 35 | 50 | 30 | 30 | 90000 |
| 4 axle rigid | high | | 50 | 50 | 90 | 90 | 15000 |
| | medium | | 40 | 40 | 80 | 80 | 15000 |
| | low | | 20 | 20 | 40 | 40 | 15000 |
| 3 axle articulated | high | | 45 | 85 | | 85 | 30000 |
| | medium | | 30 | 55 | | 55 | 30000 |
| | low | | 20 | 35 | | 35 | 30000 |
| 3 axle rigid | high | | | 60 | 90 | 90 | 15000 |
| | medium | | | 55 | 70 | 70 | 15000 |
| | low | | | 40 | 40 | 40 | 15000 |
| 2 axle rigid | high | | | 50 | | 85 | 170000 |
| | medium | | | 30 | | 35 | 170000 |
| | low | | | 15 | | 15 | 180000 |
| | | | | | | Total = | 999500[1] |

(1) There are also 500 'special' vehicles.

**TABLE 2.2     ANNUAL FLOW OF HEAVY GOODS VEHICLES (HGV)**

| | Category of road | | Annual traffic flow (millions of HGVs) | |
| *Type* | *Carriageway layout* | *No of lanes per carriageway* | *Each slow lane* | *Each adjacent lane* |
|---|---|---|---|---|
| Motorway | Dual | 3 | 2 | 1.5 |
| Motorway | Dual | 2 | 1.5 | 1 |
| All purpose | Dual | 3 | 1.5 | 1 |
| All purpose | Dual | 2 | 1.5 | 1 |
| Slip road | Single | 2 | 1.5 | 1 |
| All purpose | Single | 3 | 1 | not |
| All purpose | Single | 2 | 1 | applicable |
| Slip road | Single | 1 | 1 | |

negligible and they will not be considered any further. Similarly, vehicles smaller than those listed in Table 2.1, such as cars, also make an insignificant contribution to fatigue damage.

For convenience of calculation the designer often assumes each vehicle in the spectrum, regardless of type, to be represented by a Standard Fatigue Vehicle, which was derived to represent the effect of the Standard Load spectrum. It consists of a single vehicle of weight 320kN with 4 identical axles (Fig. 2.1) spaced 1.8, 6.0 and 1.8m apart. This approach is generally conservative compared to the application of the Standard Spectrum, although it has not been proved to be so for all joints in orthotropic decks. Thus, given the ready availability of computers, it is preferable to apply the 'real' load spectrum to the relevant influence lines.

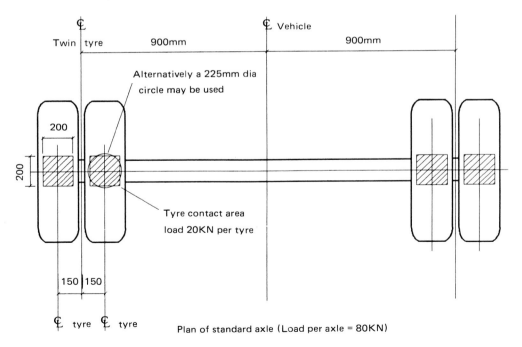

*Figure 2.1    BS 5400 Part 10, Standard Fatigue Vehicle*

9

**TABLE 2.3     COMPARISON OF PROPORTION OF VEHICLE TYPES**

| Vehicle class | TRRL class | BS 5400 | Forth Oct 1978 | Manchester road Oct 1977 | Wye Oct 1982 | M6 Feb 1978 | All roads 1981 | | | | 1985 |
| --- | --- | --- | --- | --- | --- | --- | --- | --- | --- | --- | --- |
| | | | | | | | Motorways | Class A | Class B | Class C | Motorways |
| 5 axle articulated | 42 43 54 55 5N | 3 | 0.4 | 0.4 | 0.9 | 1.6 | 37.8 | 22.2 | 7.4 | 3.6 | 13.6 |
| 4 axle articulated | 41 52 53 4N | 27 | 25.6 | 16.1 | 34.9 | 25 | | | | | 31.5 |
| 4 axle rigid | 33 35 | 4.5 | 4.7 | 0.5 | 4.1 | 2.2 | 4.5 | 4.2 | 4.2 | 3.3 | 4.5 |
| 3 axle articulated | 51 ¹/₂x3N | 9 | 5.3 | 2.6 | 4 | 6.9 | 4.3 | 3.4 | 2.4 | 1.7 | 3.5 |
| 3 axle rigid | 32 34 62 ¹/₂x3N | 4.5 | 9.6 | 4.8 | 4.3 | 5.1 | 4.4 | 5.6 | 6.2 | 6.5 | 4.3 |
| 2 axle rigid | 31 45 46 61 2N | 52 | 54.5 | 75.7 | 51.9 | 59.2 | 49.1 | 64.6 | 79.9 | 84.9 | 42.6 |

In spite of the recommendations in BS 5400 the designer may choose to use a non-standard spectrum if the Standard Spectrum is inappropriate. It is therefore of some interest to compare the Standard Spectrum with some which have been derived by observation (see Table 2.3). In this Table the 'all roads 1981' data are based on the estimated total flow of vehicles (in vehicle-kilometres) for all roads of that class in Great Britain in 1981 (9), while the 1985 motorway data represent an average for some 36 sites on the motorway network. It will be seen from these data that the two-axled rigid vehicle is the most common, followed by the four-axled articulated vehicle. However, the 'all roads 1981' data show that the proportion of four and more axled articulated vehicles is particularly high on motorways and decreases rapidly as the class of road becomes more minor.

The BS 5400 distribution is similar to that for a major road (motorway or Class A), although the proportion of three-axled articulated vehicles seems too high and, particularly following the raising of the maximum gross weight limit for articulated vehicles from 32500 to 38000 kg in May 1983, the proportion of five-axled articulated lorries seems too low. More recently, there has also been the advent of six-axled lorries. Perhaps the main, and obvious, lesson is that the proportion of each vehicle type will change with time and that, as a result, the sets of data presented here cannot be regarded as representative of present-day traffic. No doubt, at irregular intervals, the Standard Load Spectrum will have to be revised. It is notable, however, that over the period 1968-1985 the proportion of heavy goods vehicles (HGV) on major roads seems to have remained fairly constant at about 17-20%.

Similarly, traffic flow in terms of the numbers of vehicles per day has also been rising steadily and varies markedly from site to site. As far as is known, however, the flows defined in BS 5400 (see Table 2.2) still represent safe estimates.

## 2.2 Axle load spectrum

The axle load spectrum of BS 5400 is tabulated in terms of number of axles for a given axle load in Table 2.4(a) (again ignoring 'special' vehicles) and the measured spectra for four sites are given in Table 2.4(b) (omitting non-commercial vehicles). These data are plotted in Fig. 2.2 and bearing in mind the difference between the two types of data, a comparison may be made.

The BS 5400 spectrum will be seen to be 'spikier' than the measured spectra but this need not be important in terms of fatigue damage calculations. The most significant difference is that the BS 5400 spectrum contains no axle loads exceeding 100kN (the legal axle load limit in the UK), whereas 2.9% of axle loads at Forth Bridge, 2.3% at Wye Bridge and 1.0% at Manchester Road Bridge and on the M6 at Doxey exceed that limit. Obviously, if the bridge designer expects that the proportion of axles exceeding the legal limit will be significant in fatigue terms, then he should consider using a non-standard spectrum for his calculations.

A method of assessing whether the BS 5400 spectrum is comparable in fatigue damage terms to the design spectrum is to calculate the Characteristic Axle Load (CAL) of the spectrum. The CAL is the axle load which, if applied the same number of times as all the axles in the spectrum, will produce the same amount of fatigue damage. Assuming that, on account of the large number of

**TABLE 2.4 COMMERCIAL VEHICLE AXLE LOAD SPECTRA (a) BS 5400**

| Axle load (kN) | No. of axles | Percentage of axles (%) |
|---|---|---|
| 15 | 360000 | 12.62 |
| 20 | 60000 | 2.1 |
| 25 | 0 | 0.0 |
| 30 | 380000 | 13.32 |
| 35 | 320000 | 11.22 |
| 40 | 120000 | 4.21 |
| 45 | 150000 | 5.26 |
| 50 | 290000 | 10.17 |
| 55 | 165000 | 5.78 |
| 60 | 595000 | 2.09 |
| 65 | 180000 | 6.31 |
| 70 | 59000 | 2.07 |
| 75 | 0 | 0.0 |
| 80 | 59000 | 2.07 |
| 85 | 320000 | 11.22 |
| 90 | 240000 | 8.41 |
| 95 | 0 | 0.0 |
| 100 | 90000 | 3.16 |
| Totals | 2852500 | 100 |

11

**TABLE 2.4     COMMERCIAL VEHICLE AXLE LOAD SPECTRA (b) MEASURED DATA**

| Axle load (kN) | Forth Bridge Sep-74 | | Manchester Road Bridge | | Wye bridge Sep-78 | | Motorway (M6) Aug-81 | |
|---|---|---|---|---|---|---|---|---|
| | No. in range | Percent (%) | No. in range | Percent (%) | No. in range | Percent (%) | No. in range | Percent (%) |
| 0-5 | 15 | 0.15 | 7 | 0.13 | 2034 | 1.76 | | |
| 5-10 | 244 | 2.52 | 104 | 1.97 | 4295 | 3.71 | 42 | 0.84 |
| 10-15 | 324 | 3.34 | 315 | 5.98 | 2739 | 2.36 | | |
| 15-20 | 511 | 5.27 | 547 | 10.38 | 5976 | 5.16 | 349 | 6.97 |
| 20-25 | 709 | 7.31 | 688 | 13.06 | 10728 | 9.26 | | |
| 25-30 | 802 | 8.27 | 592 | 11.23 | 11382 | 9.82 | 788 | 15.73 |
| 30-35 | 810 | 8.36 | 498 | 9.45 | 10523 | 9.08 | | |
| 35-40 | 898 | 9.26 | 473 | 8.98 | 9450 | 8.15 | 789 | 15.75 |
| 40-45 | 869 | 8.96 | 444 | 8.43 | 8616 | 7.43 | | |
| 45-50 | 748 | 7.72 | 407 | 7.72 | 8878 | 7.66 | 881 | 19.58 |
| 50-55 | 645 | 6.65 | 231 | 4.38 | 7877 | 6.80 | | |
| 55-60 | 517 | 5.33 | 164 | 3.11 | 6721 | 5.80 | 801 | 15.98 |
| 60-65 | 409 | 4.22 | 125 | 2.37 | 5303 | 4.58 | | |
| 65-70 | 351 | 3.62 | 86 | 1.63 | 3916 | 3.38 | 443 | 8.84 |
| 70-75 | 316 | 3.26 | 100 | 1.90 | 3211 | 2.77 | | |
| 75-80 | 302 | 3.12 | 128 | 2.43 | 2979 | 2.57 | 342 | 6.83 |
| 80-85 | 328 | 3.49 | 149 | 2.83 | 3060 | 2.64 | | |
| 85-90 | 241 | 2.49 | 68 | 1.29 | 2505 | 2.16 | 289 | 5.77 |
| 90-95 | 213 | 2.20 | 49 | 0.93 | 1824 | 1.57 | | |
| 95-100 | 151 | 1.56 | 42 | 0.80 | 1263 | 1.09 | 235 | 4.69 |
| 100-105 | 122 | 1.26 | 22 | 0.42 | 869 | 0.75 | | |
| 105-110 | 62 | 0.64 | 13 | 0.25 | 574 | 0.50 | 40 | 0.80 |
| 110-115 | 43 | 0.44 | 8 | 0.15 | 422 | 0.36 | | |
| 115-120 | 35 | 0.36 | 6 | 0.11 | 270 | 0.23 | 10 | 0.20 |
| 120-125 | 9 | 0.09 | 3 | 0.06 | 175 | 0.15 | | |
| 125-130 | 3 | 0.03 | 1 | 0.02 | 111 | 0.10 | 1 | 0.02 |
| 130-135 | 5 | 0.05 | | | 72 | 0.06 | | |
| 135-140 | 2 | 0.02 | | | 47 | 0.04 | | |
| 140-145 | | | | | 36 | 0.03 | | |
| 145-150 | | | | | 16 | 0.01 | | |
| >150 | | | | | 19 | 0.02 | | |
| Totals | 9694 | 99.99 | 5270 | 100.01 | 115891 | 100 | 5010 | 100 |

cycles for which a bridge has to be designed, the stresses in a surfaced deck will nearly all be below the 'bend' in the S-N curve, the CAL can be calculated from the expression:

$$CAL = \frac{\sqrt[5]{\Sigma n L^5}}{\Sigma n}$$

where     n = number of axles in a load class
              L = mid range of that load class.

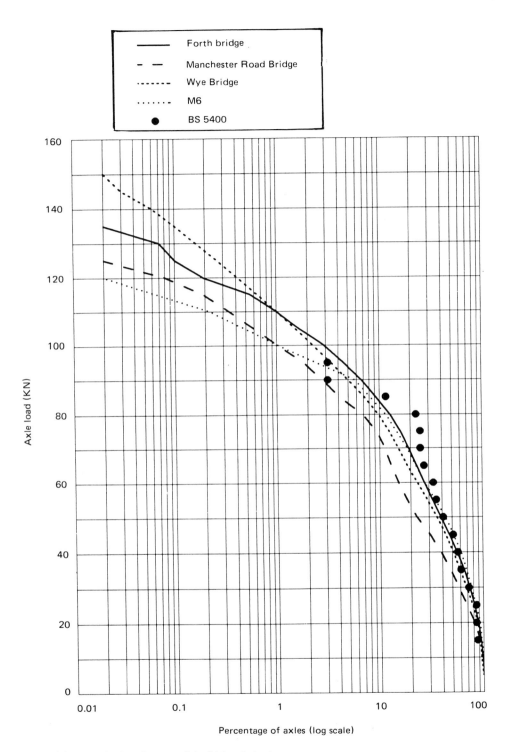

*Figure 2.2    Distribution of commercial vehicle axle loads*

13

The following values were obtained:

CAL = 69.2kN (BS 5400 'Construction & Use' vehicles)
= 67.0kN (Forth Bridge, slow lane)
= 58.7kN (Manchester Road Bridge)
= 65.1kN (Wye Bridge, slow lane)
= 64.9kN (M6 at Doxey).

The difference between the Standard Load Spectrum and the measured spectra for these sites appears therefore not to require the use of a non-standard spectrum for design.

In passing it will be noted from Table 2.4(b) that in some cases the maximum axle load was more than 1.5 times the legal limit, but this is not purely a British problem. Corresponding measurements in Europe have typically shown the legal limit to be exceeded by anything between 25 and 62%.

## 2.3 Relative contribution of front and rear wheels to fatigue

BS 5400 states that the damage done by single-tyred wheels (i.e. front wheels) is normally less than 4% of the damage done by double-tyred wheels (i.e. rear wheels) for the Standard Vehicle Spectrum. However, because front wheels have single tyres and rear wheels normally have twin tyres, a front wheel may produce higher stresses in an orthotropic deck than a more heavily loaded rear wheel.

This effect was studied by modelling the passage of 100 identical two axled lorries over a particular bridge and deriving the stress histories (at 2 positions on the underside of the deck plate) using the influence lines for the front and rear wheels respectively. (Note that the transverse influence lines for single and twin-tyred wheels have different shapes - see, for example, Fig. 3.8).

The transverse distribution of vehicle positions on the bridge was assumed to be that used in BS 5400 centred on the measured central position of commercial vehicles on the bridge. Thus a stress cycle could be deduced for each wheel, the magnitude of the cycle depending on its transverse position. The various cycles were then assembled into two stress histories, with the cycles arranged in different orders. These were chosen in such a way as to give the most, and the least, damage as assessed by use of the Reservoir method to count the stress ranges ($\sigma_r$) and hence to derive the corresponding values of $\Sigma n\sigma_r^5$. In order to be able to compare the values of $\Sigma n\sigma_r^5$ for the front and rear wheels, each value was divided by $\Sigma nL^5$, where L represents the wheel load. The results are summarised in Table 2.5.

Adjacent to the longitudinal stiffeners therefore, the front wheels produce, for equal loads, between 30 and 40 times the potential fatigue damage of the rear wheels, and clearly the contribution of the front wheels should be carefully considered for steel bridge decks.

**TABLE 2.5    RELATIVE DAMAGE DUE TO FRONT AND REAR WHEELS**

| Gauge position | $\Delta n \sigma_r^5 / \Sigma n L^5$ | | | | $\dfrac{(\Delta n \sigma_r^5 / \Sigma n L^5)\ \text{Front}}{(\Delta n \sigma_r^5 / \Sigma n L^5)\ \text{Rear}}$ | |
| | Front wheel (single tyre) | | Rear wheel (twin tyres) | | | |
| | Least damage | Most damage | Least damage | Most damage | Least damage | Most damage |
| Adjacent to stiffener | 0.0917 | 0.418 | 0.00296 | 0.0105 | 31.0 | 39.8 |
| Midway between stiffeners | 0.195 | 0.219 | 0.0427 | 0.0466 | 4.56 | 4.71 |

## 2.4    Lateral distribution of wheel loads

For the fatigue assessment of orthotropic decks it is also necessary to know the lateral distribution of wheel loads not only between traffic lanes but also within a lane. Considering first the distribution between lanes, it was proposed by Hollis and Evans that the mean hourly lane flow distribution of heavy vehicles (HGVs) on a two-lane motorway could be expressed as:

$$\text{Flow in left - hand lane} \ = \ \frac{AQ}{A + Q}$$

$$\text{Flow in right - hand lane} = \frac{Q^2}{A + Q}$$

where    Q = total flow (HGV's per hour)
A = a constant having a value of 1200.

By way of example, the mean hourly flows of commercial vehicles for the two lanes of the Wye bridge, for one week in 1978, are plotted in Fig. 2.3 against total flow. For these data, a value of A = 1350 gives a better fit to the results.

The total number of vehicles (HGV and non-commercial) at the Wye bridge for the particular five-day period considered was 15,626. The left-hand lane carried 68.9% of these (19.1% HGV and 49.8% non-commercial) and the right-hand lane 31.1% (2.6% HGV and 28.5% non-commercial). Thus, as far as HGV's were concerned, there were 88% in the slow lane and 12% in the fast lane. These proportions are very similar to those which have been found elsewhere on the M4 and on the M1 (Fig. 2.4). It will be seen that the proportion of HGV's in the fast lane of a three-lane carriageway was extremely small.

Since stresses are very sensitive to wheel position it is also necessary to consider the lateral distribution within a traffic lane. A summary of the measured positions of the offside rear wheels of commercial vehicles on 3 bridges is shown in Fig. 2.5. Normal curves may be fitted to the data, as shown in Fig. 2.6, and the mean distance from the outer edge of the lane and the standard deviation (s.d.) of the calculated curves are as shown in Table 2.6. It will be noted that the distributions about the mean paths are very similar for the 3 bridges, even though there were quite wide variations in the position of the mean path.

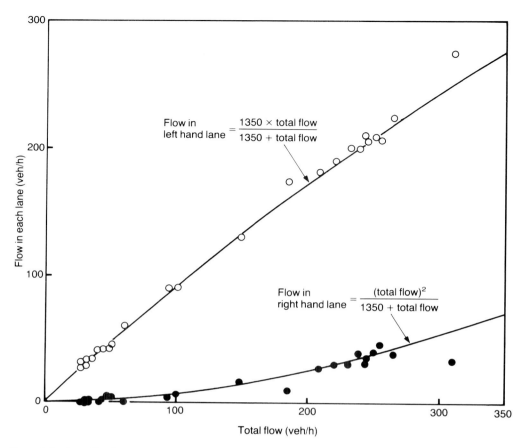

*Figure 2.3   Lane distribution of commercial vehicles: Wye Bridge (14,15 & 18-20 Sept 1978)*

These mean values show that traffic at the Forth bridge travels about 300mm closer to the centre of the carriageway than at the Wye bridge. The difference is probably due to drivers' reactions to the layout of the carriageway. The Forth bridge carriageway has a substantial kerb, joined to a strong steel grid rising at an angle of about 45°, but through which can be seen the Firth more than 50m below. The Wye bridge has a low kerb and a tensioned cable safety barrier, and the footpath or cycle path restricts the view of the river. The edge layout of the right-hand lanes of the two bridges is similar to that of their left-hand lanes, so that traffic in the right-hand lane of the Forth bridge probably travels closer to the centre-line of the carriageway than at Wye bridge.

In passing, it will be seen from Fig. 2.6 that the transverse distribution of wheel positions specified in BS 5400 is in quite good agreement with the measured values.

**TABLE 2.6    MEANS AND STANDARD DEVIATIONS OF THE TRANSVERSE WHEEL POSITIONS**

| *Bridge* | *Mean dist. from outer edge of lane (mm)* | *s.d. (mm)* |
|---|---|---|
| Wye | 894 | 238 |
| Forth | 592 | 219 |
| Manchester Road | 716 | 250 |

16

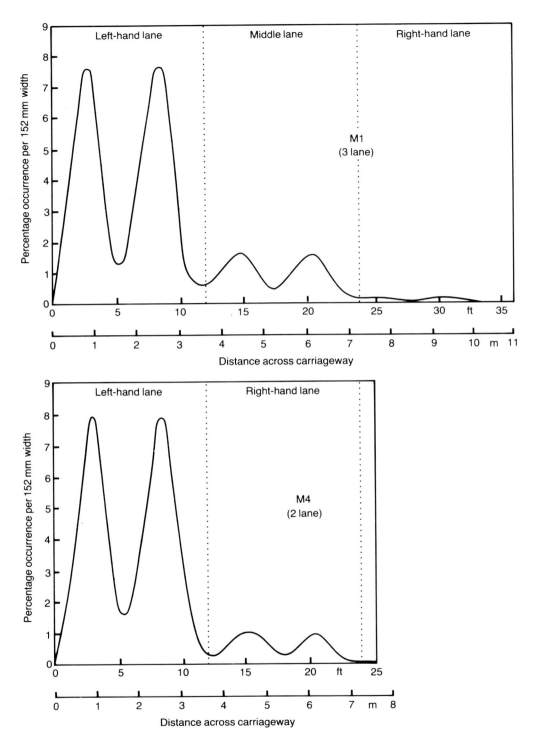

*Figure 2.4    Typical lateral positioning of commercial vehicle wheel units across a carriageway*

17

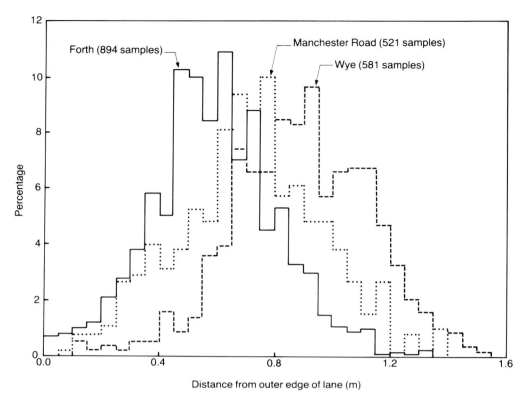

*Figure 2.5   Transverse distribution of centre lines of offside rear wheels of commercial vehicles*

## 2.5   Traffic flow in relation to time

In order to have any chance of taking account of the influence of the surfacing it is necessary, since the composite action of the surfacing is a function of temperature, to know how traffic is distributed in relation to temperature. In effect this means that it is necessary to know the distribution of traffic with respect to time of day, since traffic flow is not uniform. The effect of temperature is discussed further in Chapter 5.

Clearly this distribution will vary somewhat from site to site. As can be seen from Figs 2.7 and 2.8, which show the measurements of commercial vehicle flows at two bridges over a period of one week, the traffic flow at Manchester Road (Isle of Dogs, London) reaches a peak in the late morning, while the peak flow on the Severn Crossing occurs much earlier (0700 - 0800 hours); the flow pattern on the Forth bridge was very similar to that at Severn.

Although of no great importance from the fatigue point of view, it may be noted that the flow of non-commercial traffic on the Wye bridge was quite different to that of the commercial vehicles, with a morning peak at 0800 - 0900 hours and an afternoon peak at 1600 - 1800 hours.

18

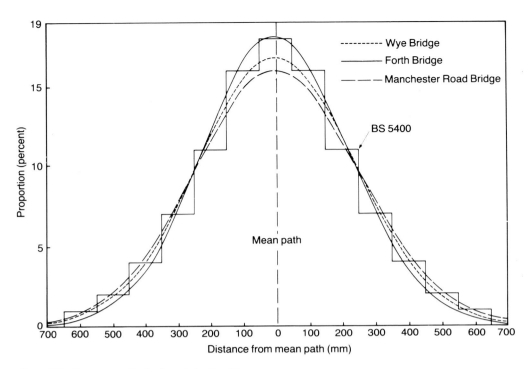

Figure 2.6    Transverse distribution of wheel positions

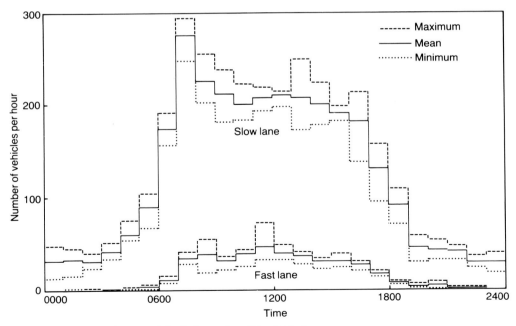

Figure 2.7    Number of commercial vehicles per hour (Wye Bridge)

19

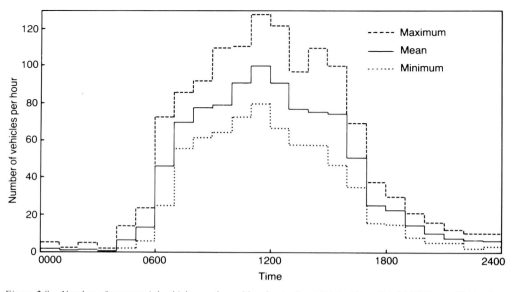

Figure 2.8    Number of commercial vehicles per hour, Manchester Road Bridge (Mon-Fri, 21-25 Nov & 28 Nov-2 Dec 1977)

# 3 STRESS DISTRIBUTIONS

Given that the loading is 'known', any fatigue assessment depends upon being able to derive from the loading the stress spectrum relevant to the particular joint under consideration. With this end in view, a very large number of influence lines were derived experimentally during the course of the project. It is clearly impossible to present them all here but it may be helpful to give some typical examples. For consistency they all relate to a deck of the same geometry as that used for the Severn Crossing (see Fig. 7.6) and, except where otherwise noted, they were derived by applying a single 20 kN load through a tyre with a contact envelope 185mm wide and 235-249mm long. This type of tyre is commonly used on commercial vehicles.

Although the results are largely self-explanatory and require few additional comments it is convenient to consider each joint in turn. Subsequently some consideration is given to the influence on these stresses of the fact that the traffic is, predominantly, in motion.

## 3.1    Longitudinal butt weld in the deck plate (Fig. 3.1)

For this joint the longitudinal influence line was very short, showing that each axle will produce its own stress pulse. Similar measurements made on other deck geometries showed almost identical influence lines for a deck with triangular, rather than trapezoidal, troughs of the same size. Similarly, for a deck with smaller but more closely spaced trapezoidal troughs the general shape of the influence lines remained the same but the magnitude of the stresses was decreased. Thus, in comparison with the peak stress of 101N/mm2 shown in Fig. 3.1 for 304mm wide troughs spaced 304mm apart, the corresponding peak stress for a deck with 279mm wide troughs spaced 203mm apart was reduced to about 64N/mm2.

## 3.2    Cross-beam to deck joint (Figs. 3.2 and 3.3)

It will be seen that, both for stresses in the deckplate and in the cross-beam, the stresses peak very sharply as a wheel crosses the cross-beam and also that the influence line is relatively short. This implies that the stresses caused by successive wheels will not usually interact with each other so that each axle will cause a cycle. In the cross-beam this cycle will alternate between tension and compression while in the deckplate there will effectively be two cycles; by rainflow counting there is a minor cycle equal to approximately 25% of the range of the major cycle caused by each wheel.

From the transverse influence lines it is clear that stresses of opposite sign, with a peak magnitude of approximately 15% of the main peak stresses, can occur if the wheel is situated over the trough rather than between troughs.

21

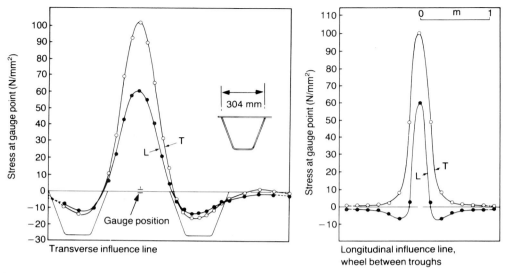

*Figure 3.1    Influence lines relating to longitudinal butt weld in deck*

### 3.3    Trough to cross-beam joint (Figs. 3.4 to 3.6)

This type of joint was rather different from most of the others in that the longitudinal influence lines relating both to the trough soffit and to the cross-beam immediately under the trough were somewhat longer. This implies that the stresses at those points are likely to be affected simultaneously by more than one axle and, particularly in the case of the trough soffit, those stresses are likely to be additive (but primarily compressive).

A deck with triangular, rather than trapezoidal, troughs gave almost identical influence lines.

### 3.4    Trough to deck joint (Figs. 3.7 and 3.8)

In comparison with the influence lines for most of the other joints, those for this particular joint are somewhat more complicated. As far as the web of the trough is concerned it will be seen that the stress may be either tensile or compressive depending upon whether the wheel is over the trough or between troughs. This implies that vehicles following each other at slightly different transverse positions can generate high stress ranges as derived by rainflow counting. On the other hand the stress in the underside of the deck plate tends to be primarily compressive regardless of whether the wheel is over the trough or the gap. For both positions, the longitudinal influence lines are short, which shows that each axle will produce a stress cycle.

However the passage of a single vehicle can give unexpected results, particularly as the twin-tyred rear wheels are usually offset laterally from the single-tyred front wheel. The results obtained for a two-axled vehicle with single front wheels and twin rear wheels on the Wye bridge deck are shown in Fig. 3.8.

22

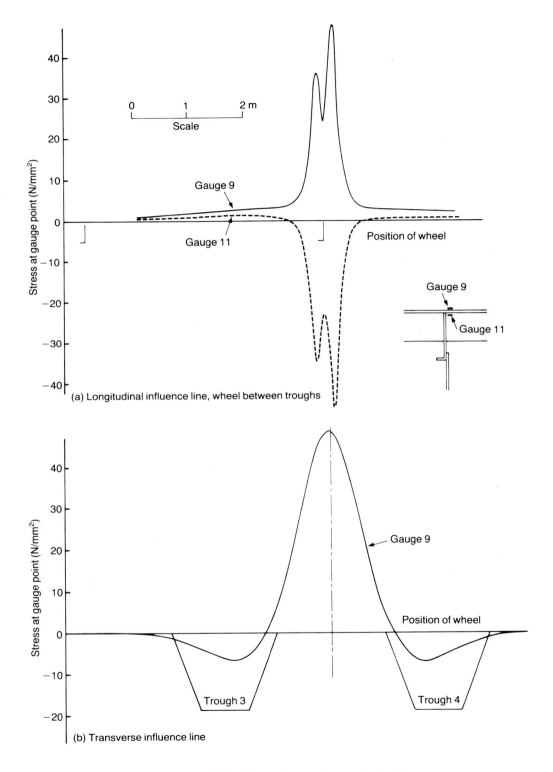

*Figure 3.2    Influence lines for stress in the deck plate at the cross-beam to deck joint*

23

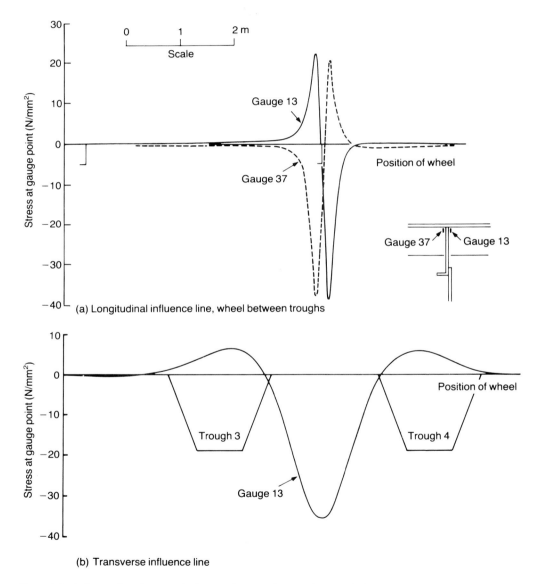

*Figure 3.3  Influence lines for stress in the cross beam at the cross-beam to deck joint*

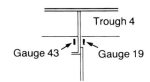

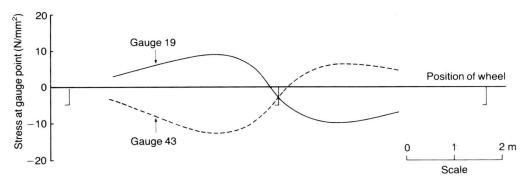

*Figure 3.4    Longitudinal influence lines for stress in the cross-beam at the trough to cross-beam joint, wheel on centre line of trough*

Comparative tests were also carried out on decks with more closely spaced troughs and also with V shaped rather than trapezoidal troughs. In both cases the general form of the influence lines was very similar to those in Fig. 3.7. However it was notable that, as in the case of the longitudinal butt weld in the deck, closer spacing of the troughs tended to reduce stresses. In this instance the transverse stress ranges, both in the deck plate and in the trough web, were approximately 25% lower in the deck with 279mm wide troughs spaced 203mm apart than in that with 304mm wide troughs spaced 304mm apart.

## 3.5    The effect of the motion of traffic on stress

While the calculated stresses for a structure are essentially 'static' stresses, those of concern to fatigue calculations are induced by moving traffic and may therefore be described as dynamic stresses. The stress measured at a particular point in a bridge structure due to a moving wheel or vehicle load is likely to differ from the stress that would occur if that load were applied at a very low speed (effectively statically - this stress should equal the calculated stress provided the method of calculation is adequate). The difference between the static and dynamic stresses is due to three main causes, namely impact, oscillation and the influence of the road surfacing. It is convenient to consider them separately.

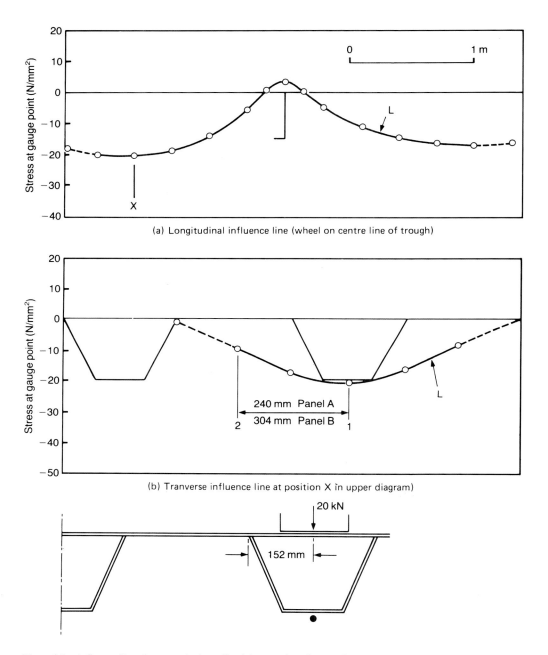

(a) Longitudinal influence line (wheel on centre line of trough)

(b) Tranverse influence line at position X in upper diagram)

Figure 3.5   Influence lines for stress in the soffit of the trough at the trough to cross-beam joint

26

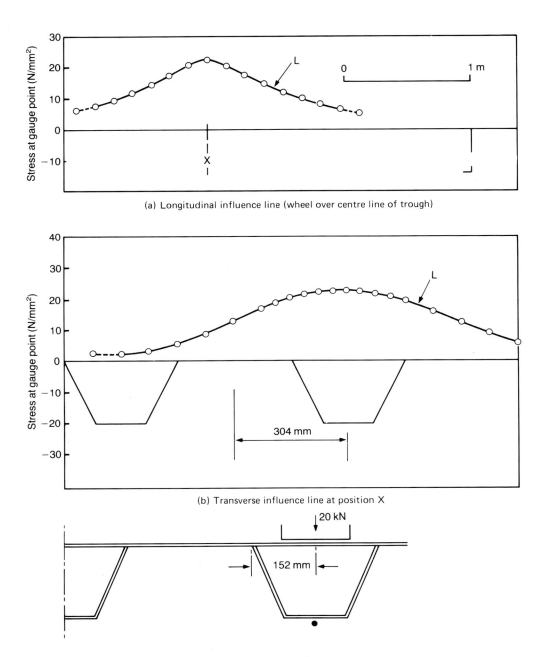

Figure 3.6 *Influence lines for stress in the soffit of the trough midway between cross-beams*

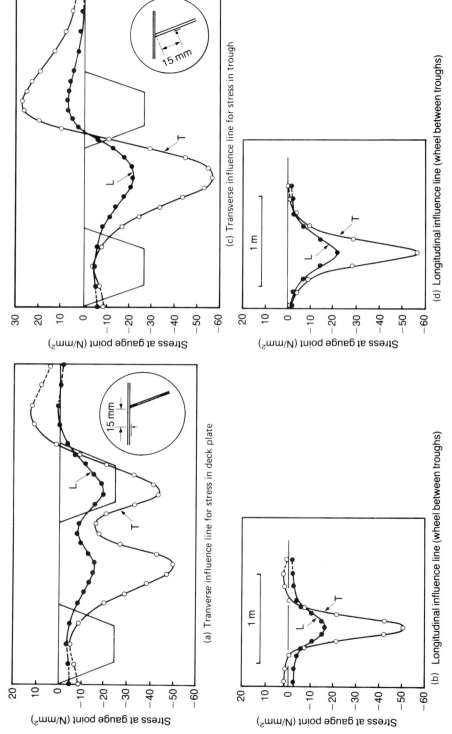

Figure 3.7 *Influence lines relating to the trough to deck joint*

28

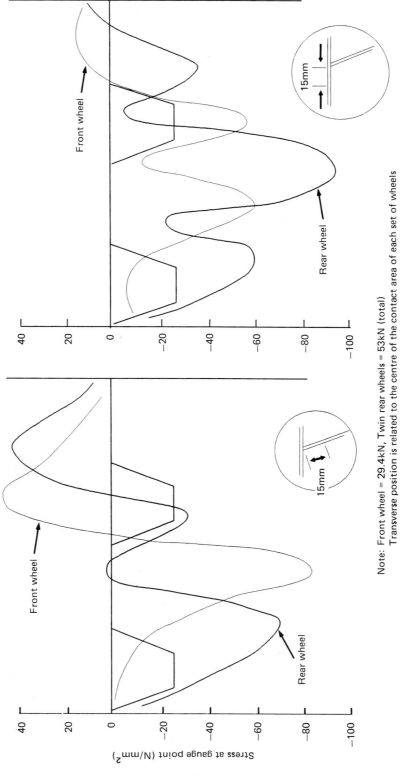

Note: Front wheel = 29.4kN, Twin rear wheels = 53kN (total)
Transverse position is related to the centre of the contact area of each set of wheels

*Figure 3.8   Transverse influence lines for stress at trough to deck joint at longitudinal positions of maximum stress (two axle test vehicle on Wye Bridge)*

### 3.5.1 Impact

If the road or bridge surface is perfectly smooth, straight and horizontal, then a vehicle travelling along it will apply constant loads to the surface through its tyres - its static wheel loads. In practice, this condition never occurs because all road and bridge surfaces have irregularities which excite the vehicle and cause dynamic variations about the static wheel load. The effect of these variations is likely to be most important in relation to the bridge deck.

Measurements made with a test vehicle on several motorway bridges at a speed of 48km/hour showed upper values of impact factor ranging from 1.11 to 1.47 (there will of course also be values less than 1.0 due to the vehicle 'pitching'). Although 48km/hour is a low speed for a motorway, previous measurements had shown that the dynamic wheel load was only likely to increase very slightly at higher speeds. Nevertheless, it is clear from the small sample of bridges used in these tests that stresses in parts of the bridge structure will be considerably higher than those derived from the static values of wheel load and that an allowance must be made for dynamic effects in fatigue design.

Another method of investigating the influence of surface irregularities, given that bridges tend to have various joints which occur at regular intervals along their lengths, is to measure strains at nominally identical positions on several of these joints. In this particular investigation this was done for the trough to deck joint, the strain gauges being situated adjacent to the same trough in adjacent bays and only 4.3m apart longitudinally. It therefore seemed reasonable to expect the stress spectra measured at these two positions to be directly comparable. The two spectra which were measured, in the course of approximately 50 hours, were as shown in Fig. 3.9, and calculations showed that the fatigue damaging effect of one is about four times that of the other. This difference is large and it certainly suggests that data from a single gauge should be treated with great caution.

Although it was not possible to determine the precise reason for the difference in this particular case, possible reasons seem to be:

i)    different dynamic components of wheel load when the wheel is longitudinally above each gauge, due to road surface irregularities;

ii)   differences in thickness and/or stiffness of the asphalt surfacing, together with variations in composite action due to varying bond between the surfacing and the deck;

iii)  differences in the gauge position relative to the weld;

iv)   differences in plate thickness, weld dimensions, or fit-up of the welded plates.

From the design point of view it is relevant to note that, for short influence lines, where individual axle loads are important, BS 5400 increases the axle loads by 10% to allow for their variability compared to the spectrum of gross vehicle weights. BS 5400 also makes an allowance for impact where a discontinuity occurs in the road surface (for example at an expansion joint) when the static stress at every point affected by a wheel, at or within 5m of the discontinuity, is increased by magnifying the relevant influence line.

30

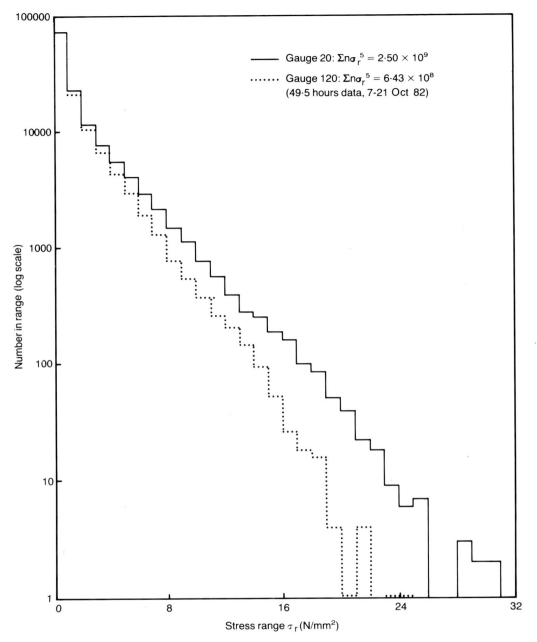

*Figure 3.9    Histograms of stress range measured by two gauges situated 4.3m apart longitudinally (Wye Bridge)*

The measurements made in the course of this work suggest that the highest values of impact occur close to a discontinuity, particularly the start of the bridge. However, these peak impacts are in many cases considerably higher than the design allowance, as are the peaks away from the discontinuity. These measurements confirm that any design allowance should be in two parts, an overall allowance for the whole bridge plus an additional allowance in the vicinity of any surface discontinuity built into the bridge.

31

### 3.5.2 Oscillation

Even if the bridge surface is perfectly smooth so that no load variations occur because of surface irregularities, the load applied by the vehicle as it enters the bridge will deflect the bridge dynamically, so that it will begin to vibrate, which in turn will cause the vehicle to oscillate, thus producing further load variations in the bridge. This will produce variations of stress in the structure about the stress that would occur if the load were applied statically.

The analogue tape recordings of strain obtained in the course of this work were examined to find periods where the passage of a vehicle was followed by oscillations of the strain record, and reservoir counts of the cycles were carried out for some typical records. As a result it was found that, assuming fatigue damage is proportional to the fifth power of stress range, the stresses due to vibration account for only $3.5 \times 10^{-5}$ per cent of the total fatigue damage potential and may therefore be neglected.

It is conceivable that vibrations could make a significant contribution in the case of a bridge with a natural frequency in the region of that due to body bounce (generally 2-4Hz) or axle hop (generally 10-15Hz) of commercial vehicles. The fundamental bending mode natural frequency of the Wye bridge, for example, is 0.46Hz.

### 3.5.3 Influence of road surfacing

Many steel bridges are surfaced with asphalt whose material properties are viscoelastic. This has the effect of reducing the stresses in the structure for a moving load compared with the same load applied statically. Again, this effect is of particular importance to the deck structure, and the whole question of the influence of surfacing is considered in some detail in Chapter 4.

# 4  DECK SURFACING

## 4.1  Introduction

The asphalt surfacing normally applied to steel decks has three main purposes:

i)    to provide a running surface with suitable skid resistance, etc;
ii)   to provide a flat running surface by varying its thickness to compensate for distortions of the steel deck plate;
iii)  to protect the deck plate by providing a waterproofing layer.

It is therefore an essential part of the structure. However, in addition, it has the advantage of reducing traffic induced stresses in the deck structure by acting compositely with the deck plate. On the other hand it is necessary to bear in mind its weight. In the Severn Crossing, for example, the weight of the surfacing is approximately 20% of the total suspended weight of the structure. If this could have been reduced there would have been a consequent saving of weight on the cables, towers and foundations, so in some respects it is desirable that the surfacing should be as thin as possible. Nevertheless it is notable that bridges in UK have tended to have thinner surfacings than corresponding bridges in the rest of Europe.

It also has to be remembered that a steel deck is more flexible than concrete, so the surfacing has to accommodate greater deflections without cracking. This conflicts with the requirement for high stiffness to give good wearing properties and the bonus - since it is not included in design - of reducing stresses in the steel by composite action.

However in this context there are other problems, since the properties of asphalt are both viscoelastic and temperature dependent and they may also change as the asphalt ages, so the reduction in stresses is very variable. This is in fact one of the main reasons why its contribution is not normally taken into account for design purposes. At present therefore the surfacing provides a factor of safety of unknown magnitude. If the contribution of the surfacing could be quantified it might be possible to take it into account for design purposes, thus leading to a more efficient and hence cheaper structure, although adequate maintenance (including replacement) would be necessary to ensure that its contribution remained effective through the life of the bridge.

Before going on to consider the work which was carried out to investigate the effect of the surfacing it may be helpful briefly to summarise the form of surfacing which has been employed.

In general, the surfacing system is made up of a number of components, not all of which may be needed for a particular application:

i)    waterproofing layer to protect the steel.
ii)   tack coat for adhesion between waterproofing layer and wearing course.
iii)  the wearing course.
iv)   a non-skid surface dressing (not relevant to this trial).

Thus there is a flexible interface between the steel and the wearing course which results in partial composite action.

Steel decks on long span bridges in the UK have traditionally been surfaced with hand laid mastic asphalt. This provides a good, durable surface with good rutting resistance and satisfactory resistance to fatigue cracking, but it is slow to apply compared to machine laying, and this increases traffic disruption. In addition there is a growing shortage of operators with the necessary skills, as machine laying has taken over for most applications other than bridges. Unfortunately standard hot rolled asphalt is not really suitable for steel decks because of sensitivity to fatigue cracking and inadequate adhesion. Long span bridges are such a small market that there is little incentive to develop the required techniques to overcome these problems, although it is interesting to note that machine laid mastic was used on the Humber bridge, but the experiment has not been repeated. At the time of writing, the Severn Crossing is being resurfaced with hand laid mastic asphalt.

In passing, it may be noted that mastic asphalt is a composite material which consists essentially of a bituminous binding medium called asphaltic cement, or binder, mixed with a finely graded aggregate. To this mixture a percentage of coarse aggregate is added, the grading and amount of which is governed by the thickness at which the mastic is laid. Since mastic asphalt is voidless, it is not mechanically compacted as are such materials as rolled asphalt and macadam.

The main difference between mastic asphalt and rolled asphalt is that mastic asphalt contains roughly twice as much binder. This increase in binder content provides the flexibility necessary to accommodate the expansions and contractions imposed by the bending of the deck plate under wheel loads. To keep permanent deformation or rutting within reasonable bounds a much more viscous binder is also used. This is typically achieved by using a blend of Trinidad Lake Asphalt (TLA) and a petroleum based bitumen.

Epoxy hot rolled asphalt and polymer modified mastic asphalt have been mentioned as possible improvements on standard mastic asphalt. Indeed, epoxy asphalt has been produced with the required properties and machine laid on a bridge deck; in fact trial panels have been laid on the Severn and Erskine bridges as well as on the North bound carriageway of the Forth Bridge. However, performance has been very variable. In general there is little experience in the UK with this material and the requirements for preparation and delivery are very stringent. It is also more affected by low ambient temperature during laying. The effectiveness of the composite action is also less well known. Thus, as mastic asphalt has been proved by many years of experience to be reasonably satisfactory from the points of view of performance, production and laying, there would probably need to be very convincing reasons before a switch to a different material would be considered. It might well be that, if the cost of delays to traffic during re-surfacing were incorporated in the evaluation of alternative systems, a different conclusion might be recorded. It is interesting to note, for example, that the French are investing heavily in machine laid systems.

## 4.2    Influence of surfacing on deck stresses

In view of the situation outlined above various attempts were made to quantify the effect of the surfacing on the stress at several of the welded joints which occur in orthotropic decks. This included the derivation of influence lines for various joints both with and without surfacing together with a limited study of the influence both of the temperature of the surfacing and of vehicle speed. In addition comparisons were made of different types of surfacing, particularly epoxy and mastic asphalt.

The initial tests to study the influence of the surfacing were carried out on the Denham panels (Fig. 1.4). These involved deriving influence lines for a range of vehicle speeds and for various points on the deck structure. The results showed:

(i)     that the surfacing had a negligible effect on the stress at the soffit of the trough but could have a large effect on the stresses closer to the deck plate;

(ii)    that the stress at the trough to deck joint, on the underside of the deck, was not affected significantly by the 9mm epoxy surfacing but that it was greatly reduced by the composite action of a 38mm mastic asphalt surface (see Fig. 4.1). Admittedly those two sets of results were obtained with slightly different speeds, temperatures and wheel loads, but the differences are not so great as to nullify the validity of the comparison.

(iii)   The transverse influence lines for the panel with mastic asphalt surfacing (Fig. 4.2), which relate to the nearside rear wheels only and which are plotted relative to the centre of the twin wheel unit, show a marked effect of vehicle speed. The greatest reduction in transverse strain occurred between static loading and with the vehicle moving at a very slow speed (less than 1km/hour), but there were further reductions as the speed increased.

The longitudinal strains (Fig. 4.2b) do not show the same changes with vehicle speed. The dynamic influence line shows both reductions and increases in the strain depending on the transverse position of the vehicle wheels. The effects are small in magnitude but are similar for speeds up to 16km/hour. The changes in the measured strains are probably due to a redistribution of stress under the wheels because the dynamic stiffness of the surfacing is greater transverse to the weld line than in the longitudinal direction, because of differences in the rates of straining.

Subsequent to the work on the Denham panels, comparative influence lines were obtained for a range of joints both with and without surfacing and some typical examples are shown in Figures 4.3 - 4.5. They all relate to a deck surfaced with hand laid mastic asphalt with the test vehicle passing over it at 32km/hour (20mph). This was considered, on the basis of earlier work, to be a speed at which most of the strain reduction would have occurred but since, in practice, most vehicles would be travelling at higher speeds the stresses might actually be still lower. Hence the measurements were expected to give conservative (i.e. low) estimates of fatigue life.

Comparison of the results for the 3 joints shows that, in all cases, the strains were greatly reduced by the presence of the surfacing although the magnitudes of the reductions did vary between joints. Thus, at 11-14°C surfacing reduced the stress by between about 70 and 83%. At the higher temperature of 37-41°C the reduction was considerably less (between 43 and 63%). This shows

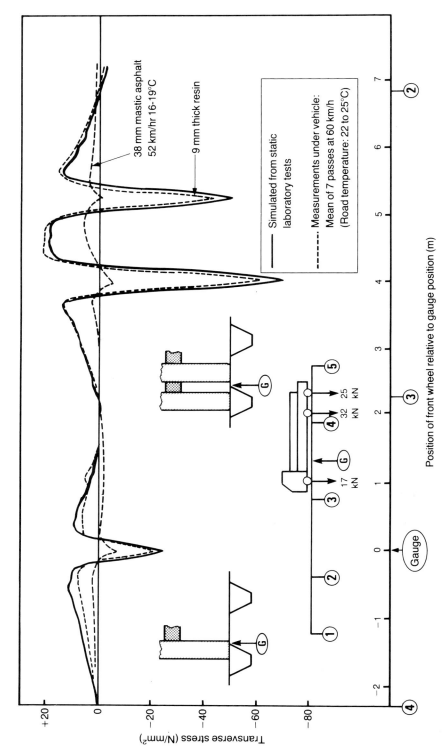

Figure 4.1   Comparison between static and dynamic longitudinal influence lines for stress at trough to deck joint

36

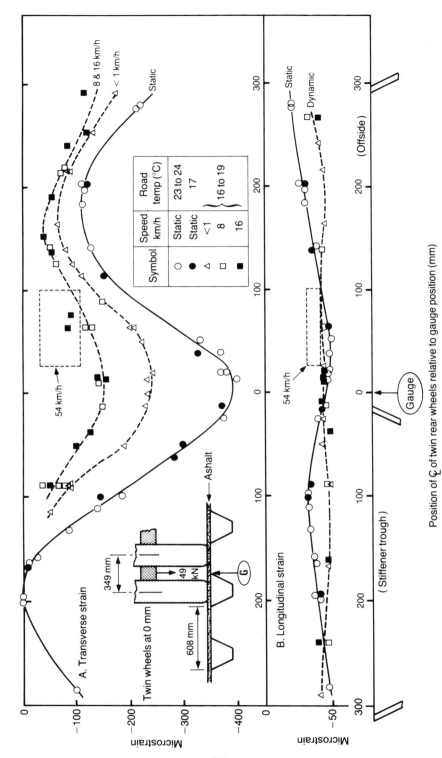

Figure 4.2 *Transverse influence lines showing relationship between vehicle speed and strain at trough to deck joint*

37

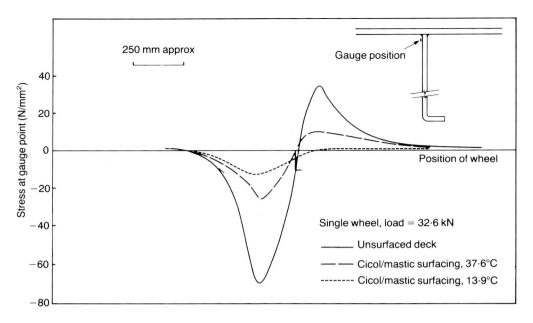

*Figure 4.3    Longitudinal influence lines for stress in cross-beam at cross-beam to deck plate joint*

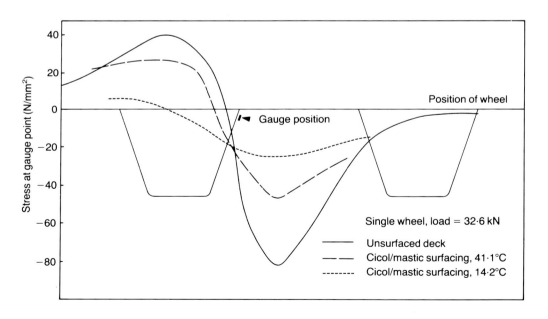

*Figure 4.4    Transverse influence lines for stress in trough at trough to deck plate joint with and without surfacing*

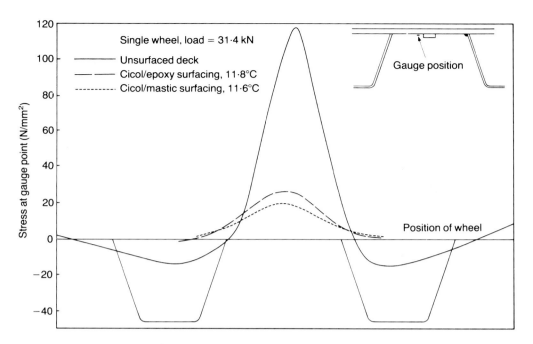

*Figure 4.5    Transverse influence lines for stress in deck plate at longitudinal butt weld with and without surfacing*

conclusively that surfacing temperature is, potentially, an important variable. The tests also showed (Fig. 4.5) once again that the stress can be sensitive to the type of surfacing which is used.

In order further to study the influence of surfacing type, comparative measurements were made over a period of about two years on two sections of the deck of the Severn Crossing, one with an epoxy asphalt surfacing and one with mastic asphalt. The strains induced in several types of joints were monitored in pairs, one of each pair being situated under each type of surfacing. However as the joints in each pair were only some 10 metres apart longitudinally, and at the same transverse position relative to the traffic lanes, it was assumed that they were subjected to the same traffic loading.

During the first year, measurements were made at intermittent intervals and comparative fatigue lives were calculated assuming the slopes of the relevant S-N curves were m = 3.0. As far as the epoxy system is concerned, it was found that its effectiveness in reducing stress increased with time; this 'cure time' is characteristic of the epoxy asphalt system. Thus, disregarding the early results, when the epoxy system may not have been fully cured, the calculated life improvement ratios due to the surfacing (i.e. life of surfaced deck/life of unsurfaced deck) derived from pairs of measurements made at approximately the same date and the same surfacing temperature are given in Table 4.1.

On the basis of these results it is clear that, at similar temperatures, the epoxy system is generally less effective in reducing stresses than the mastic system. In this context it must, however, be remembered that a major difference between the two surfacing systems is the requirement for a tack coat for the epoxy system between the Cicol and the asphalt. The performance of this tack coat, particularly its cure time and post cure temperature characteristics, is therefore very

**TABLE 4.1    FATIGUE LIFE IMPROVEMENT DUE TO SURFACING**

| Position | Temperature (°C) | Life improvement ratios | | |
|---|---|---|---|---|
| | | *Mastic* | *Epoxy* | *Mastic/epoxy* |
| Trough to deck in trough | 17.4-18.1 | 15 | 8.9 | 1.68 |
| | 16.4-16.5 | 17.4 | 10.5 | 1.66 |
| Web to deck in deck | 20.6-19.9 | 7.1 | 2.6 | 2.73 |
| | 13.8 | 11.8 | 4 | 2.95 |
| | 12.4-14.8 | 2.1 | 1.7 | 1.23 |
| Crossbeam to deck in deck | 22.4-21.4 | 46.8 | 15.5 | 3.02 |
| Crossbeam to deck in crossbeam | 22.4-21.4 | 100 | 42.4 | 2.36 |
| Longitudinal butt weld in deck | 11.6-11.8 | 149 | 63.6 | 2.34 |
| | 19.0-21.8 | 124 | 39.6 | 3.13 |

important. Its performance is crucial to the composite action effect of the asphalt, since it transmits the shear forces into the steel deck. Similarly the effectiveness of the mastic system depends on a mechanical key between the asphalt and Cicol; this bond has not been subjected to long term assessment, but obviously the enhanced fatigue lives noted above depend upon it remaining in good condition throughout the life of the surfacing system.

Subsequently, in the second part of the trial the strains at the various joints were monitored continuously, under normal traffic, for a period of 13 months and a summary of some of the results which were obtained is shown in Table 4.2. In most of the joints the stresses under the 38mm machine laid epoxy asphalt were again higher than those in the deck with the same thickness of mastic asphalt, although the reverse was true of the trough to cross-beam joint. This joint has, however, always proved difficult to assess since stresses measured at different joints under nominally similar conditions have varied widely. As noted previously, the tests at Denham suggested that the joint was too far from the deck plate to derive any appreciable benefit from the presence of surfacing, although these later measurements did show that, in fact, there was some benefit. Detailed analysis of the results for the trough to deck joint and for the longitudinal butt weld showed no significant change in the relative effects of the two surfacings over the 13 month period of the trial.

Throughout this experiment measurements were also made of the temperature of the surfacing and a theoretical assessment was made of the amount of fatigue damage which occurred at each temperature. It was found that the temperature was only above 20°C for 17% of the time, although most of the fatigue damage occurred in that regime. Of the damage which occurred, the calculated percentages which were amassed above 20°C are given in Table 4.3.

The effect of surfacing temperature is shown more clearly in Figs. 4.6 and 4.7. Dividing the 'fatigue damage', as calculated using Miner's rule, by the time in each temperature band gives an indication of the *rate* of usage of fatigue life. It will be seen that relatively little 'damage' occurs below 15°C, but above this the rate rises, especially for the deck coated with epoxy surfacing. At 30°C the rate of accumulation of fatigue damage of the longitudinal butt weld with an epoxy surfacing is ten times the rate for the same joint with mastic surfacing. The surfacing temperature is only above 30°C for 4% of the time but this accounts for up to 54% of the 'damage'. The transition region between 15°C and 30°C is also important in comparing the two surfacings.

40

TABLE 4.2

**TABLE 4.2    SUMMARY OF STRESS RANGE HISTOGRAMS MEASURED AT VARIOUS JOINTS IN A PERIOD OF 13 MONTHS (JULY 1985 - AUGUST 1986)**

| Stress range (N/mm²) | *Total no of stress cycles* | | | | | | | |
|---|---|---|---|---|---|---|---|---|
| | Longitudinal butt weld | | Crossbeam to deck | | Trough to deck | | Trough to crossbeam | |
| | *Mastic* | *Epoxy* | *Mastic* | *Epoxy* | *Mastic* | *Epoxy* | *Mastic* | *Epoxy* |
| 8-12 | 215,729 | 266,893 | 42,104 | 61,952 | 240,778 | 268,874 | 57,994 | 194,601 |
| 12-16 | 215,705 | 157,522 | 13,889 | 19,323 | 145,105 | 171,957 | 226,828 | 72,634 |
| 16-20 | 53,999 | 103,595 | 3,368 | 6,097 | 90,542 | 109,116 | 139,319 | 27,551 |
| 20-24 | 17,815 | 54,081 | 1,219 | 2,408 | 55,652 | 64,266 | 90,353 | 8,116 |
| 24-28 | 6,511 | 25,738 | 488 | 1,194 | 28,224 | 33,297 | 58,676 | 1,770 |
| 28-32 | 2,814 | 14,067 | 174 | 624 | 12,799 | 15,711 | 40,929 | 481 |
| 32-36 | 1,204 | 8,334 | 87 | 315 | 6,322 | 7,653 | 28,340 | 99 |
| 36-40 | 587 | 5,505 | 28 | 150 | 3,277 | 4,148 | 19,267 | 16 |
| 40-44 | 207 | 3,523 | 10 | 77 | 1,841 | 2,540 | 13,088 | |
| 44-48 | 133 | 2,372 | 5 | 26 | 1,096 | 1,667 | 8,362 | |
| 48-52 | 78 | 1,526 | | 16 | 746 | 1,172 | 4,761 | |
| 52-56 | 26 | 1,035 | | 4 | 445 | 857 | 2,420 | |
| 56-60 | 8 | 585 | | 3 | 304 | 625 | 1,190 | |
| 60-64 | 6 | 371 | | 1 | 202 | 457 | 592 | |
| 64-68 | 0 | 246 | | | 125 | 333 | 303 | |
| 68-72 | 2 | 134 | | | 79 | 212 | 182 | |
| 72-76 | 1 | 101 | | | 46 | 158 | 93 | |
| 76-80 | 1 | 54 | | | 27 | 93 | 50 | |
| 80-84 | 1 | 37 | | | 12 | 73 | 19 | |
| 84-88 | | 14 | | | 10 | 45 | 9 | |
| 88-92 | | 8 | | | 1 | 20 | 4 | |
| 92-96 | | 2 | | | 4 | 13 | 1 | |
| 96-100 | | 0 | | | 1 | 9 | | |
| 100-104 | | 1 | | | 0 | 3 | | |
| 104-108 | | 1 | | | 1 | | | |
| 108-112 | | | | | | | | |
| 112-116 | | | | | | | | |
| Totals | 421,926 | 645,745 | 61,372 | 92,190 | 587,639 | 683,299 | 692,779 | 302,268 |

**TABLE 4.3    FATIGUE DAMAGE AT SURFACING TEMPERATURES ABOVE 20°C**

| Joint | Fatigue damage (%) | |
|---|---|---|
| | *Mastic* | *Epoxy* |
| Trough to deck joint | 57 | 66 |
| Longitudinal butt weld | 74 | 85 |

The rise in the rate of 'fatigue damage' with temperature is not due to higher HGV traffic flow when the surfacing is hotter. In this particular case it was calculated that only 19% of the HGV traffic passed while the temperature was above 20°C or 33% while it was above 15°C. Below 15°C there is little difference in composite action between the mastic and epoxy surfacings and the rate of fatigue damage is low.

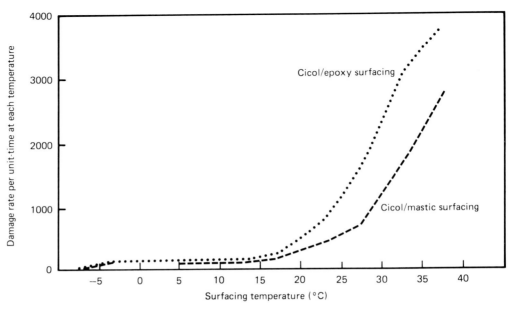

*Figure 4.6    Variation of the rate of fatigue damage with temperature for the trough to deck joint*

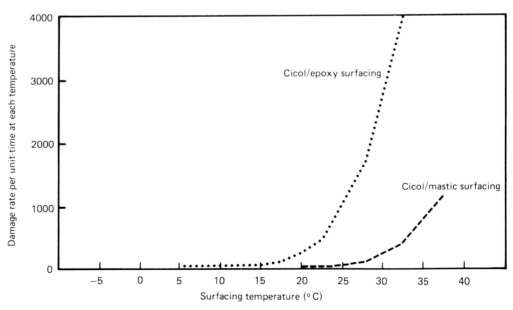

*Figure 4.7    Variation of the rate of fatigue damage with temperature for the longitudinal butt weld in the deck plate*

## 4.3   Fatigue strength of the surfacing

As noted previously, mastic asphalt has been shown by experience to be reasonably satisfactory for bridge decks. Nevertheless, fatigue cracking has occurred both in the asphalt surfacing and in the welded deck structure in some bridges.

As far as fatigue cracking of the asphalt is concerned, the problem is usually associated with hard spots in the deck. For example (Fig. 4.8) a double tyred lorry wheel straddling the trough web causes a hogging bending moment in the deck and the tensile stresses in the asphalt can lead to longitudinal fatigue cracking in the surfacing.

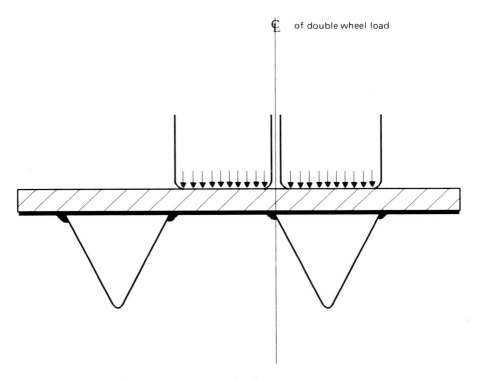

Figure 4.8   *Load producing hogging moment over trough web*

Hence, in view of the cost and disruption of repair work there was a considerable incentive to improve structural performance. As a result various attempts were made to increase the durability of the surfacing and also its stiffness, since a stiffer asphalt mix would increase the stiffness of the deck and reduce the stresses in the welded joints.

Given the fact that mastic asphalt had been proved, by experience, to be reasonably satisfactory, experiments were carried out with various mix designs, with particular reference to binder content and viscosity, to see if there was an optimum mix. The control mix was essentially similar to that adopted for surfacing the Humber Bridge. In the alternative mixes a high viscosity binder was achieved by using 100% TLA while the low viscosity binder comprised 100% of 50 pen bitumen. The control mix was a 50:50 blend of each.

43

D

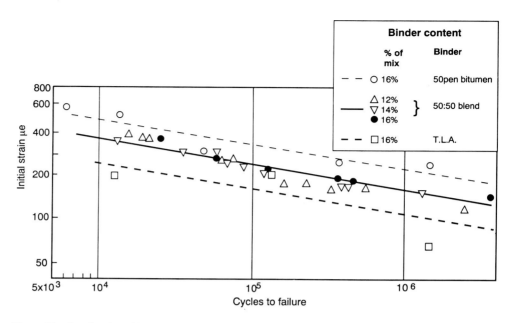

*Figure 4.9    Results of axial load fatigue tests on mastic asphalt*

The results of axial load fatigue tests on the various mixes are summarised in Fig. 4.9. The inferior performance of the 100% TLA mix may stem from its greater stiffness. The most significant result, however, was that a mix with a low viscosity binder gave a better fatigue performance than the 50:50 blend of 50 pen bitumen and TLA.

However, since viscosity and binder content have a marked effect on the stiffness of mastic asphalt there was some doubt as to which would perform better when acting semi-compositely with a steel deck. The stiffness of the 100% 50 pen binder was about half that of the 50:50 blend. Thus in a bridge deck, under identical wheel load, larger strains would be expected. This might well counter the apparently better fatigue life when expressed in terms of initial strain. Conversely, the greater stiffness of the 100% TLA mix may make up for its inferior strain performance. Thus there was no certainty as to whether flexural fatigue performance would be improved by a more viscous or a less viscous binder.

Tests were therefore carried out under 3 point bending on specimens with six different mixes of asphalt. They consisted of 12.7mm steel plates with a 40mm layer of asphalt, the asphalt being in tension. Most of the specimens were tested at the same load but at different temperatures and it was found that, for each mix, there was a distinct minimum in the endurance curve corresponding to a 'worst' temperature (Fig. 4.10). This varied between 15°C and 25°C according to the type of mix.

In the first three mixes (4, 14 and 24, Fig. 4.10) binder viscosity was varied while other factors were held constant. In mixes 1 and 6 the soluble binder content was varied and the final mix (no. 10) was based on the most favourable indications from the previous tests. It was found that reducing the binder viscosity improved the fatigue life at temperatures above 13°C but reduced

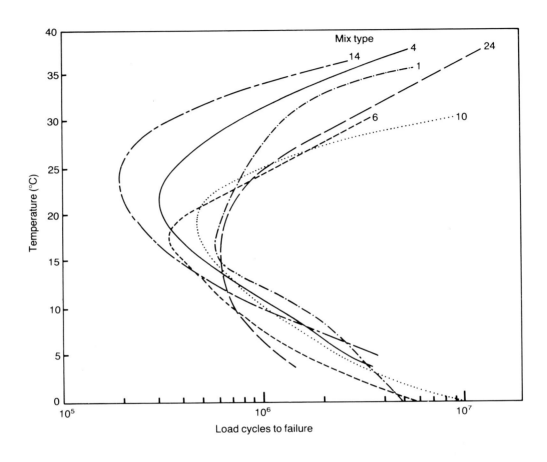

| Mix type | TLA | Binder content % | | % soluble binder in mortar | |
| | | 50 pen bitumen | 15 pen bitumen | | |
| --- | --- | --- | --- | --- | --- |
| 4 | 50 | 35 | 15 | 15 | 'Control' mix |
| 14 | 67 | 23 | 10 | 15 | High viscosity |
| 24 | 33 | 67 | — | 15 | Low viscosity |
| 1 | 50 | 35 | 15 | 13 | Low binder content |
| 6 | 50 | 35 | 15 | 17 | Higher binder content |
| 10 | 33 | 67 | — | 13 | 'Optimum' mix |

*Figure 4.10  Influence of temperature on the fatigue life of asphalt covered steel plates under three point bending*

it at lower temperatures. A leaner mix improved the fatigue life above 15°C and made little significant difference below. The best result was achieved with a lean mix using a low viscosity binder. This resulted in a considerably longer fatigue life than the standard mix above 13°C while below that temperature there was little significant difference.

On a balance of the properties, in terms of stiffness and endurance to fatigue cracking, it was concluded that the optimum mix for asphalt was 33% TLA, 67% 50 pen bitumen with the soluble binder content equal to 13% of mortar, and that little further improvement would be obtainable using traditional binder constituents. In practice these properties would be most reliably ensured with the mastic asphalt laid unchipped, in which case the necessary skid resistance would have to be provided by an additional treatment. The eventual choice of mix for a particular application will obviously be influenced by its workability and resistance to deformation.

## 4.4    The effect of cracks in the asphalt

A potential problem with relying on the composite action of the asphalt surfacing to reduce the applied stresses is that as noted previously, the asphalt may crack. When this does happen it usually occurs over a 'hard spot', such as the connection between a stiffener and the deck plate, and one might reasonably expect such cracking to result in loss of effectiveness of the surfacing.

In order to assess its significance some tests were carried out on part of the Severn Bridge at a location where the asphalt surfacing appeared to be uncracked and in good condition. Strain gauges were installed on the underside of the deck plate midway between the troughs, representing the position of a longitudinal butt weld in the deck, and also adjacent to a trough to deck joint. They were then used to derive influence lines both for the uncracked surfacing and for a 'cracked' surfacing, the cracks being simulated by making 35mm deep sawcuts in the asphalt.

Some typical results are shown in Figs. 4.11 - 4.13. As far as the transverse stress midway between troughs is concerned it will be seen from Fig. 4.11 that the 'cracking' rather more than doubled the stress as compared with that for a deck with an uncracked surface, but the stress was still only about 40% of that for an unsurfaced deck. By far the greatest part of the stress increase occurred on making the longitudinal crack directly over the gauge position. In the case of the longitudinal stress at the same position, however, it was found that 'cracking' caused a total loss of effectiveness of the surfacing, the stresses in the deck with cracked surfacing being the same as in an unsurfaced deck.

Turning now to the trough to deck connection, the compressive peak stress in the trough (Fig. 4.12) was increased, as a result of 'cracking' of the surfacing, by about 50% as compared with that in the deck with the uncracked surface and, again, most of this increase occurred when a longitudinal 'crack' was made directly over the joint. The stress was, however, still very much lower than that in an unsurfaced deck. In the deck, however, the stress (Fig. 4.13) was more than doubled by cracking, but it remained well below the unsurfaced value, although it was interesting to note that, for a wheel directly over the joint, the stress in the presence of cracked surfacing was similar to that in an unsurfaced deck, but of opposite sign.

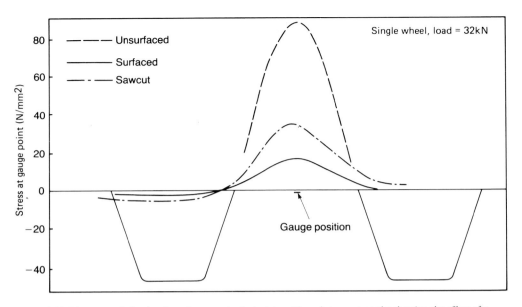

*Figure 4.11  Transverse influence lines for stress in deck plate midway between troughs showing the effect of a simulated crack in the surfacing*

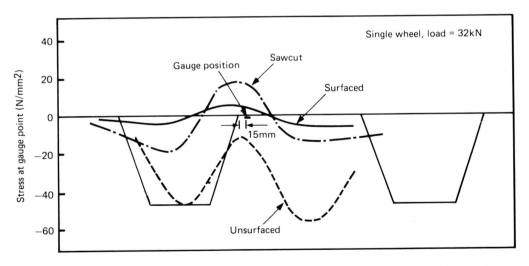

*Figure 4.12  Transverse influence lines for stress in the deck plate adjacent to the trough to deck joint, showing effect of a simulated crack in the surfacing*

47

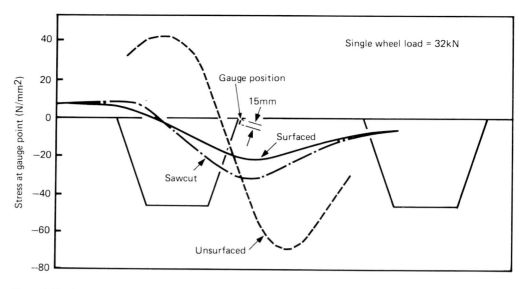

*Figure 4.13 Transverse influence lines for stress in the trough adjacent to the trough to deck joint, showing effect of a simulated crack in the surfacing*

In summary, therefore, this work confirmed that conventional asphaltic bridge deck surfacings in good condition significantly reduce stresses in the welded connections near the deck plate caused by wheel loads from vehicles. However, cracks in the surfacing do tend to reduce its effectiveness and stresses in the steel then increase. For some connections the loss of effectiveness is small and the stresses under cracked surfacing are still significantly less than those measured on an unsurfaced deck. For other connections the loss of effectiveness is total. In general, the largest increases in stress are usually associated with a crack directly over the connection in question.

It follows that, if surfacing were to be relied on over long periods to reduce stresses in the welded connections of orthotropic bridge decks so as to provide an acceptable fatigue life, a lower bound stress reduction factor representing cracked surfacing would need to be determined for each connection. Extensive experimental trials would be required to obtain these factors. It would also be necessary to develop NDT methods to check the composite action over the life of the surfacing.

48

# 5  SURFACING TEMPERATURE

It has been noted previously that, as a result of composite action with the deck plate, the surfacing can have a large effect on the stresses in some of the joints that exist in orthotropic decks. However the stiffness of the surfacing varies with temperature so that, in order to be able to derive more accurate stress spectra, it is also necessary to have information on temperature variations.

Such information is also relevant to the potential use of epoxy resins for bonding reinforcement plates to a structure, since it has been shown that the fatigue performance of a bonded joint is affected by the subsequent levels of temperature experienced by the joint. In particular it has been shown that the fatigue performance is sensitive to temperatures above 45°C, and also that the static strength of the joint is at a maximum at about 30°C. Because of this temperature dependence, any fatigue assessment must take into account not only the actual levels of temperature likely to be experienced by the joint during the expected life of the bridge, but also the lengths of time the joint will be at those levels.

In general, the temperature of a bridge is governed by the effects of all three of the processes of heat transfer, namely conduction, convection and radiation. During the day the greatest part of the energy available for heating comes from the sun in the form of short wave, high temperature solar radiation. At the road surface of a bridge some of this incident radiation is lost by reflection, some by convection and some by long wave, normal temperature re-radiation; the remainder is absorbed into the deck of the bridge. The amount of reflected radiation is dependent on the colour and texture of the surface: light-coloured, or shiny uneven surfaces will reflect a much larger amount of radiation than a matt, flat black surface, and the latter will reach a much higher temperature. The amount of energy lost by convection and re-radiation is dependent on the wind speed, the exposure of the surface and the difference in temperature between the surface and the surrounding air.

The remaining heat energy is conducted down through the deck of the bridge and changes its temperature. The speed with which the heat is conducted is dependent on the diffusivity of the materials of construction. (The diffusivity, $K$, is related to the thermal conductivity, $k$, the density, $p$, and the specific heat, $c$, by the equation $K = k/pc$.)

The undersurface and all other exposed surfaces of the bridge receive (or lose) heat from the long wave, normal temperature radiation from (or to) the surroundings. The amount of heat exchanged is again dependent on the wind speed, the exposure of the various surfaces and the differences in temperature between the surfaces and the surrounding air (i.e. the shade temperature). However the heat input to these other surfaces is unlikely to have more than a local effect on the temperature of a large steel deck plate.

During the night heat is lost from the structure by re-radiation. On clear nights the 'radiation temperature' of the night sky can be as low as -40°C, and the loss of heat from an exposed horizontal surface, such as the road surface of a bridge, can be large enough to reduce the surface temperature below that of the surrounding air. Heat is also lost (or gained) by convection and re-radiation at the exposed surfaces of the bridge and by conduction from within the deck. As for the daytime conditions, the amount of heat exchanged is dependent on the wind speed, the exposure of the surfaces and the differences in temperature between the surfaces and the surrounding air.

Since the radiation, wind speed and shade temperature are variable quantities, the distribution of temperature through the depth of the deck of a bridge is complex. For example, Fig. 5.1 shows the temperatures within the deck of a steel box bridge during a 24-hour period of good weather in the summer, while Fig. 5.2 shows the corresponding values for a period including a clear cold winter night.

The temperature distributions in Fig. 5.1 show that the areas nearest to the road surface reach the highest temperatures, have the largest daily ranges of temperature and reach their maximum temperature first. (The temperatures of the surfacing materials are not included.) The greater the distance from the upper surface, the lower and later are the maximum temperatures reached. With a thin deck plate and a diffusivity about 20 times higher than that of concrete, the steel temperature rises very quickly to temperatures well in excess of the shade temperature. Similarly Fig. 5.2 shows that, near the road surface at night, the temperatures are, for some of the time, lower than that of the surrounding air. The minimum effective bridge temperature was usually found to occur during, or close to, the period 06.00 ±1 hour G.M.T.

In view of the obvious potential importance of the temperature of the surfacing, measurements were made of the temperature spectra at mid-depth of the surfacing at four sites. The results, expressed in terms of the percentage of time the surfacing temperature was within specific 5°C

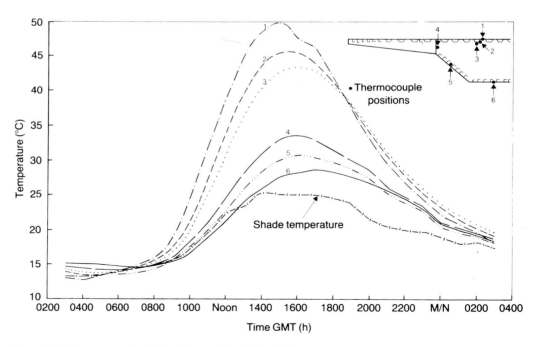

Figure 5.1   Temperature distribution for a steel box bridge in Summer

50

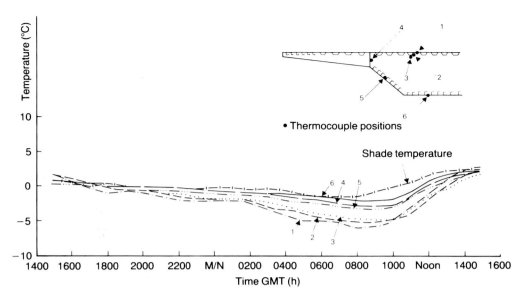

*Figure 5.2    Temperature distribution for a steel box bridge in Winter*

intervals, are summarised in Table 5.1. Although, as might be expected, there were differences between the various sites, it was notable that, at any particular site, there were no significant year to year differences for the two years over which the measurements continued and it does seem possible to draw some conclusions.

In the first place, the measurements at Denham clearly provide a direct comparison between epoxy and asphalt surfaces. They show that, at least in that instance, the epoxy surfacing reached a higher maximum temperature (54°C) than the asphalt (49°C). This difference is probably due primarily to the fact that the temperatures were measured at mid-depth of the two surfacings, so

**TABLE 5.1      PERCENTAGE OF TIME IN EACH TEMPERATURE RANGE AT MID DEPTH OF SURFACING**

| Temperature range (°C) | Denham asphalt 1969 | 1970 | Denham epoxy 1969 | 1970 | Severn Bridge 1967 | 1968 | Wye Bridge 1/3/69 to 28/2/70 | 1/3/70 to 28/2/71 | Sutton Bridge 17/3/66 to 15/3/67 | 26/3/67 to 23/3/68 |
|---|---|---|---|---|---|---|---|---|---|---|
| -10 to -5 | 0.06 | 0.08 | 0.0 | 0.06 | 0.0 | 0.05 | 0.55 | 0.23 | 0.25 | 0.61 |
| -5 to 0 | 2.71 | 1.99 | 1.14 | 2.97 | 2.39 | 1.96 | 8.33 | 6 | 7.06 | 10.84 |
| 0 to 5 | 15.96 | 13.53 | 16.18 | 13.81 | 9.77 | 13.19 | 20.68 | 48 | 24.21 | 22.21 |
| 5 to 10 | 22.45 | 24.03 | 26.22 | 23.31 | 30.57 | 24.14 | 25.91 | 18.21 | 27.46 | 26.37 |
| 10 to 15 | 15.51 | 19.64 | 17.00 | 21.56 | 22.33 | 18.89 | 19.04 | 25.09 | 22.3 | 20.07 |
| 15 to 20 | 19.84 | 19.64 | 16.98 | 17.43 | 17.12 | 16.37 | 12.63 | 23.33 | 11.84 | 11.74 |
| 20 to 25 | 11.43 | 9.39 | 8.61 | 7.39 | 7.98 | 10.87 | 6.59 | 11.81 | 5.11 | 5.48 |
| 25 to 30 | 5.70 | 5.29 | 5.75 | 5.07 | 4.66 | 7.57 | 3.50 | 7.19 | 1.43 | 2.18 |
| 30 to 35 | 3.22 | 3.77 | 3.58 | 3.82 | 2.71 | 3.86 | 1.71 | 4.01 | 0.31 | 0.44 |
| 35 to 40 | 1.88 | 1.90 | 2.16 | 2.39 | 1.73 | 2.05 | 0.87 | 2.49 | 0.04 | 0.05 |
| 40 to 45 | 1.11 | 0.68 | 1.47 | 1.57 | 0.59 | 0.80 | 0.2 | 0.89 | | |
| 45 to 50 | 0.14 | 0.06 | 0.81 | 0.56 | 0.14 | 0.23 | | 0.26 | | |
| 50 to 55 | | | 0.11 | 0.06 | | 0.02 | | 0.02 | | |

that, with the epoxy being thinner than the asphalt, its temperature was measured nearer the surface. However, as was to be expected, the minimum and mean temperatures were very similar for both materials (-5°C and 14°C).

Similarly one would expect the Severn and Wye bridges to give very similar results, since they are effectively adjacent to each other. In fact, however, the hourly mean temperatures at Wye were approximately 3°C lower at all times of the day. The difference may possibly have been due to the relative camber and longitudinal inclination of the deck surfaces.

Meanwhile it was found that Sutton bridge was much colder than the Denham asphalt, i.e. the maximum temperature was 10°C lower, the mean and the mean hourly temperatures were 5°C lower. Sutton bridge is 142km north of Denham on the east coast and the structure of the bridge is such that the deck is in shadow for most of the day. However the main cause of the difference is almost certainly that the structure is of open girder design, so that there would have been much greater heat losses from the undersurface of the deck plate than would have been the case in the box girder bridges.

Overall, the maximum temperatures varied from 37°C at Sutton bridge to 54°C for the Denham epoxy, and the minimum temperatures varied from -5°C for the Denham epoxy to -9°C on the Wye bridge.

The method of calculation of the temperature of an unsurfaced deck plate of a steel box section, although outside the scope of this document, has been fully described by Emerson (LR561), and applications of the method of calculation have been reported by Jones (LR560). Based on those methods, it has been shown theoretically that the 1 in 120 year maximum temperature of an 11.4mm deck plate of a steel box with 38mm of surfacing in the United Kingdom can be taken to be 65°C, with a duration unlikely to exceed one hour. Over the range of plate thicknesses likely to be used in practice (say 10-25mm) the difference in the daily maximum deck temperature is negligible (only about 1°C). On the other hand, surfacing depth has a greater effect and a reasonable empirical relationship suggests that the maximum deck plate temperature beneath the surfacing reduces by 3°C for each 20mm depth of surfacing or, going the other way, the temperature of an unsurfaced deck would be about 5°C greater than that of a deck with 38mm of surfacing.

Unlike extreme maximum or minimum values of deck plate temperatures, all intermediate temperatures can result from many combinations of environmental conditions, with particular emphasis on shade temperature and solar radiation values. It is therefore difficult to predict accurate durations of deck temperature levels. Nevertheless, an estimate was made for a hypothetical 11.4mm thick deck plate of a steel box girder bridge in the Kew area with 38mm of surfacing for the 10 years from 1962 to 1971, and it was found that the surfaced deck plate would be:

| | | |
|---|---|---|
| at or above 58°C for approximately | 1 | hour |
| at or above 57°C for approximately | 2.5 | hours |
| at or above 56°C for approximately | 3.5 | hours |
| at or above 55°C for approximately | 6 | hours |
| at or above 54°C for approximately | 11 | hours |
| at or above 53°C for approximately | 17 | hours |

| at or above 52°C for approximately | 31.5 | hours |
|---|---|---|
| at or above 51°C for approximately | 58 | hours |
| at or above 50°C for approximately | 103.5 | hours |
| Total: | 234 | hours |

In contrast, a similar analysis carried out for 8 days during the hot spell of the summer of 1976 gave an estimated total of 184.5 hours for deck plate temperatures at and above 50°C.

These two examples illustrate the variability of the British climate and help to show why it is not possible to predict, with any reliability, levels and durations of deck plate temperatures likely to be achieved over selected numbers of years.

In order to gain some indication of the magnitude of the temperature effect on fatigue damage, an assessment was made of the distribution of flow of commercial vehicles with temperature at the Wye bridge (Fig. 5.3). The associated stress and axle load spectra were then grouped according to the surfacing temperature (to the nearest 1°C) and a measure of the corresponding fatigue damage, $\Sigma n\sigma_r^5$, was calculated. (This assumes that all the stresses would be low enough

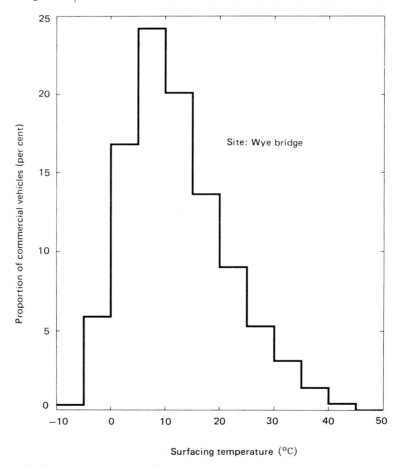

Figure 5.3   Distribution of commercial vehicle flow with surfacing temperature, Wye Bridge

to be situated on the lower branch of the relevant design S-N curve which, in BS 5400, has a slope $m = 5$.) Then, in order to be able to compare the values of $\Sigma\sigma_r^5$ for different conditions the various values were 'non-dimensionalized' by dividing by the corresponding value of $\Sigma nL^5$, where L represents the wheel load.

Some typical results which were obtained for a range of temperatures at two different times are summarised in Fig. 5.4. As expected, there is a general tendency for $\Sigma n\sigma_r^5/\Sigma L^5$ to increase with increasing temperature, and for the top surface of the deck plate (gauge 1 - see fig. 5.4) the rate of increase is extremely rapid. At low temperatures the asphalt makes a significant contribution to stiffness and the junction between the steel and asphalt is close to the neutral axis of the composite plate and thus low stresses are measured. As the temperature increases the stiffness

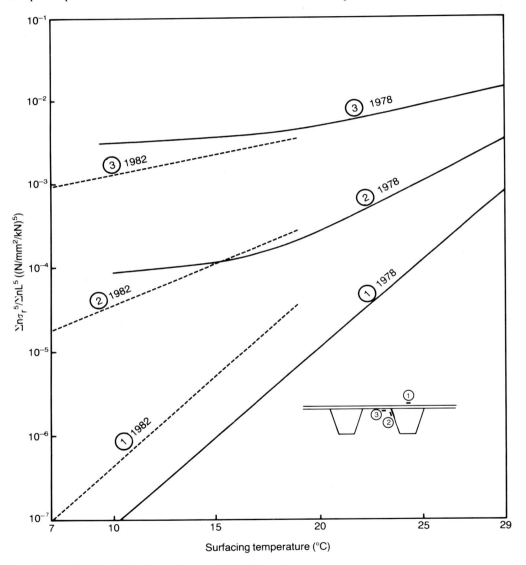

*Figure 5.4  Effect of surfacing temperature on relative fatigue damage*

of the asphalt decreases and the neutral axis of the composite plate moves towards the centre of the steel plate. At the highest temperature measured, it is probable that the asphalt is contributing very little to the overall stiffness. Although this strain gauge was not adjacent to a weld its behaviour makes it clear that the stresses at a weld on the top surface (between two plates, for instance) are highly dependent on the behaviour of the surfacing.

The gauges on the bottom surface of the deck plate (3) or attached to the trough (2) show increases in the ratio $\Sigma n \sigma_r^5 / \Sigma L^5$ of between 4 and 50 between 10 and 30°C, so the effect of temperature is also important for the stress levels at these welds.

It is interesting to note (Fig. 5.4), from a comparison of the 1978 and 1982 results, that the curves for gauges 2 and 3 appear to be a continuation of each other at 20°C, the apparent changes of slope in the 1978 curves having disappeared. This suggests that, at the lower temperatures, the asphalt became stiffer over time. On the other hand, the slope of the curve for gauge 1 did not change but the curve moved laterally, implying that the asphalt had become less stiff. Clearly further studies are required fully to explain the behaviour of asphalt.

# 6  FATIGUE TESTS ON PLATE SPECIMENS

The geometric form of an orthotropic deck, and the type of loading to which it is subjected, necessarily imply that most of the joints are subjected primarily to bending, rather than axial, stresses. However, at the start of this fatigue testing programme, there were extremely few data relating to the fatigue strength of welded joints in bending, and to some extent that is still true today, since the great majority of fatigue test results for welded joints have been obtained under axial loading. This arose from the fact that fatigue testing machine availability was limited, and it was therefore felt desirable to concentrate work on the situation which was not only likely to occur with the greatest frequency but which was also presumed to be associated with the lowest strength. Allied to this fact, design S-N curves, such as those contained in BS 5400 (Part 10), have always been based on axial loading data and it has been accepted that structures or joints subjected essentially to bending stresses, such as orthotropic decks, might therefore be somewhat overdesigned, particularly if they were thin.

Initially, interest was concentrated primarily on the strength of the trough to deck plate joint failing from the weld toe as a result of bending stresses in the deck plate. In addition such joints can be subjected to bending stresses in the weld and the stiffener, shear stresses in the weld and direct stresses in the stiffener. Hence fatigue failures could, potentially, also occur in the weld throat, with the crack initiating either at the root or the weld surface, or in the stiffener from the weld toe (Fig. 6.1). Similar failure modes were also envisaged as being possible in the trough to crossbeam joint. As a result each of these modes of failure was investigated in some tests on plate specimens, the primary objective being to obtain some basic data for joints in bending.

For ease of identification, the various types of plate specimens, details of which are shown in Figs 6.2-6.4, are designated by the identification letters Px. Whenever possible the corresponding test series is referred to by the same letters, but different series of the same general specimen type have a number in addition (e.g. PF2).

The first two types of specimen (Fig. 6.2) were concerned with the 'basic' situation of a plate with a welded stiffener present but carrying no load. All these specimens were subjected to four-point bending, specimen Type PA (with a single attachment) being tested at R = -2 at the weld toe while the specimens of Type PF (with two attachments) were tested at R = 0. The latter tests were not, in fact, directly related to the test programme on orthotropic decks but more to a general investigation of the fatigue strength of non-load-carrying fillet welded joints in bending. However, since they are, in a sense, directly comparable it is interesting to include the results at this stage.

Specimens of Types PB and PC (Fig. 6.3) were concerned with the fatigue strength of joints with a bending moment applied to the stiffener but with no bending in the main plate. Using specimen Type PB, made with a butt weld from one side, tests were carried out with the stress at the weld

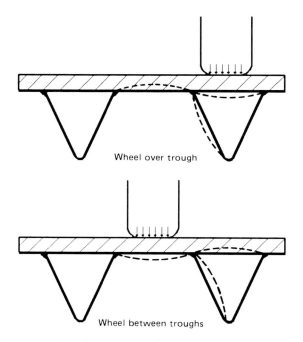

Wheel over trough

Wheel between troughs

a) Schematic modes of deformation of the joint under wheel loading

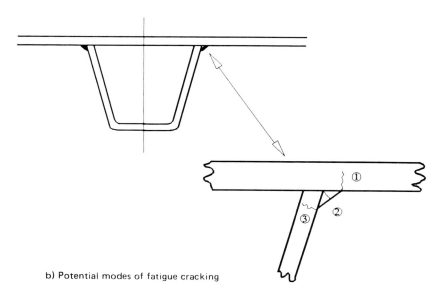

b) Potential modes of fatigue cracking

*Figure 6.1    Behaviour of the trough to deck plate joint*

57

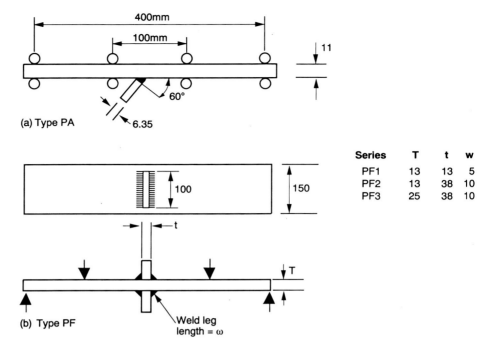

| Series | T | t | w |
|--------|-----|-----|-----|
| PF1 | 13 | 13 | 5 |
| PF2 | 13 | 38 | 10 |
| PF3 | 25 | 38 | 10 |

Figure 6.2    Specimens with unloaded stiffeners

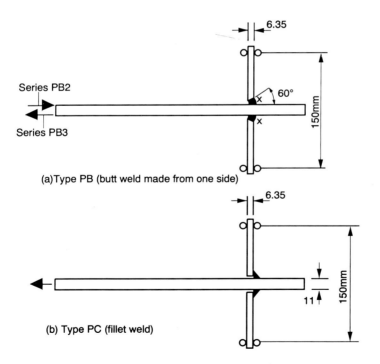

Figure 6.3    Specimens with the stiffeners in bending

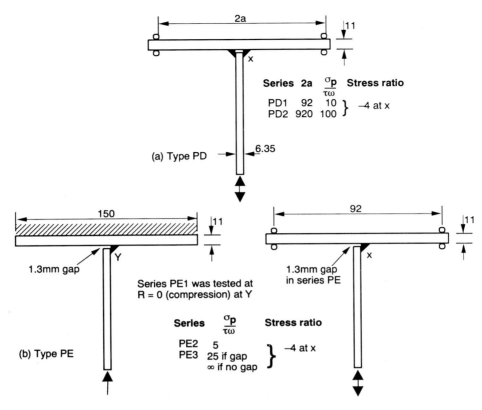

*Figure 6.4    Specimens and loading details to study interaction of shear and bending stresses*

toe both fully tensile and fully compressive, while for the fillet welded joint (Type PC) only loading giving full compression at the weld toe and tension at the root was used.

Finally, specimens of Types PD and PE (Fig. 6.4) were again concerned with a fillet welded stiffener to main plate connection and consisted of a single stiffener fillet welded at right-angles to the surface of the main plate with either one or two welds. In each case direct loading was applied to the stiffener while the main plate was subjected to bending, and by making the joints with a deliberate gap between the stiffener and the main plate it was ensured that shear stresses existed in the weld. The general objective of the tests was then to examine the influence of the interaction between the shear stress in the weld ($\tau_w$) and the bending stress in the main plate ($\sigma_p$) directly above the stiffener. Shear stresses in the weld could give rise to failure in the weld throat, while bending stresses in the plate could lead to failure in the plate at the weld toe. In an attempt to cover both cases, different values of the ratio $\sigma_p/\tau_w$ were used, as indicated in Fig. 6.4.

E

## 6.1   Failure in the main plate

Although only one test series (Series PA, Fig. 6.2) in the orthotropic deck test programme was specifically intended to produce fatigue cracking in the main plate it did in fact also occur in Series PD1 and PD2 (Fig. 6.4). However, since all these series were tested at compressive stress ratios, -2 or -4, it may be convenient to start by considering the results obtained with specimens of Type PF (Fig. 6.2), which were tested at R = 0 and which were also intended to fail in the main plate.

The relevant results are shown in Fig. 6.5, from which it can be seen that there was a distinct influence both of specimen thickness and of attachment size. Since all the S-N curves were of approximately equal slope, it is easy to make comparisons between the strengths of the three series. The same comparison can also be made for specimens of the same geometry (but stress-relieved) which have been tested under axial loading and for which the S-N curves were also approximately parallel with each other. However, it is more difficult to compare the axial loading and bending results because the two sets of results had S-N curves of different slopes.

Thus dealing first of all with the effect of joint geometry the fatigue strengths at 2 x 10⁶ cycles, and the slopes of the S-N curves, which were obtained under axial and bending stresses are given in Table 6.1.

Comparing the results for Series PF1 and PF2 it will be seen that increasing the attachment and weld sizes while keeping the main plate thickness constant leads to a substantial reduction in fatigue strength (about 10% in bending and 20% under axial loading). Equally, considering series

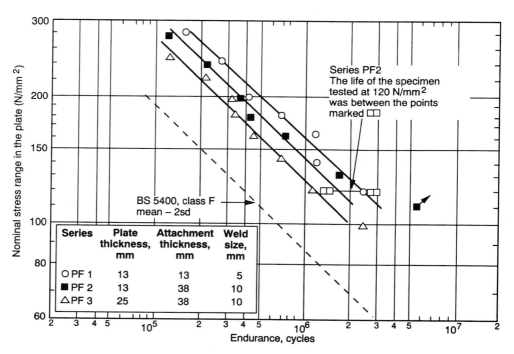

Figure 6.5    Test results for specimens with transverse fillet welds tested at R=0 in 4 point bending

60

**TABLE 6.1    FATIGUE TEST RESULTS FOR SPECIMENS FAILING IN THE MAIN PLATE.**

| Series | Geometry | Fatigue strength (N/mm2) | | Slope of curve | |
|---|---|---|---|---|---|
| | | Axial* | Bending | Axial* | Bending |
| PF1 | T=13, t=13, w=5 | 147 | 127 | -4.03 | -3.2 |
| PF2 | T=13, t=38, w=10 | 119 | 115 | -3.85 | -3.1 |
| PF3 | T=25, t=38, w=10 | 110 | 100 | -3.71 | -3.04 |

* Stress-relieved joints.

PF2 and PF3, increasing the main plate thickness while keeping the attachment and weld sizes constant also leads to a substantial reduction in fatigue strength.

Thus, on the basis of results for only two pairs of test series it appears that main plate thickness, for this joint type, is (as expected) more significant under bending than axial loading; the comparison between 13 and 25mm thick specimens shows a reduction in strength of about 15% under bending load compared with only about 7.5% under axial loading. On the other hand, attachment thickness is more significant under axial as opposed to bending stresses.

Owing to the fact that the axially loaded specimens tested previously were stress-relieved while the specimens tested under bending stress were as-welded, no valid direct comparison can be made between them as far as absolute strengths are concerned. It is, however, clear from Fig. 6.5 that all the bending test results were substantially above the Class F mean - 2 S.D. design curve. In fact, for these particular results Class D would be a more satisfactory design criterion, but as yet there are insufficient confirmatory results available for that change to be formally recommended.

Turning now to the tests under more compressive stress ratios, the results are summarised in Fig. 6.6. In order to simplify comparisons the S-N curve for Series PF1 (from Fig. 6.5) and the Class

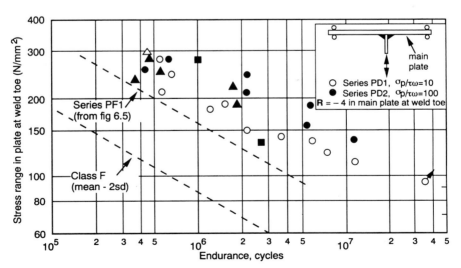

*Figure 6.6    Test results for specimens with load carrying fillet welds (series PD1 and PD2) failing in the main plate from the weld toe*

61

F mean - 2 S.D. design curve are also shown. As might be expected, both from the fact that the main and attachment plates were thinner than in Series 1 and as a result of the tests being at a more compressive stress ratio, the test results were significantly above the results obtained at R = 0 and far above the Class F design curve.

## 6.2  Failure from the weld toe in the stiffener

The main difference between the tests involving failure in the stiffener (series PB1) and in the main plate was that the stiffener was considerably thinner, so that the stress gradient was steeper. In addition the specimens were tested at R = 0 rather than at a compressive stress ratio.

The relevant results are shown in Fig. 6.7, which also shows the scatter band embracing the test results involving toe failures in the main plate (from Fig. 6.6) and the S-N curve for Series PF1 (from Fig. 6.5). Apart from the fact that the S-N curve for series PB1 is extremely flat, it is notable that the results are in good agreement with those for failure in the main plate and above those for Series PF1, which were tested at the same stress ratio but which were thicker. Indeed, when taken in conjunction with all the results for Series PF1, PF2 and PF3 (Fig. 6.5) it seems clear that Series PB1 provides further evidence of increasing fatigue strength with decreasing thickness of stressed plate.

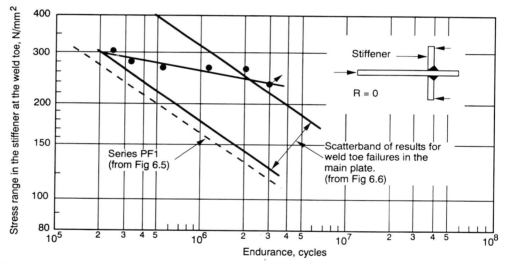

*Figure 6.7    Test results for butt welded specimens (series PB2) failing from the weld toe in the stiffener*

## 6.3  Failure in the weld throat

All the weld failures occurred under bending stresses. In Series PE1 the bending stress was wholly tensile on the weld surface and consequently cracks initiated there and propagated through the throat. In Series PB2 (with butt welds) and PC (with fillet welds) the stress was, however, wholly tensile at the weld root, so that cracks initiated at the root and then propagated through the throat. The same mode of failure also occurred in Series PE2 and PE3, even though the loading gave a greater cyclic tensile stress on the weld surface than at the weld toe. The more severe stress concentration at the root accounts for the mode of failure.

The results relating to failures from the weld surface are shown in Fig. 6.8 and from the weld root in Fig. 6.9. For ease of comparison the S-N curve for surface failures is also included in Fig. 6.9 from which it can be seen that it is considerably higher than most of the root failure results.

As in the case of Series PD1 and PD2 made with two fillet welds, there did not appear to be any significant difference in strength between Series PE2 and PE3, which were tested with different values of $\sigma_p/\tau_w$. With a single weld used to attach the stiffener to the plate, direct loading in the stiffener inevitably produced bending as well as shear stress in the welds. The bending stress turned out to be the important stress parameter. From fracture surface observations it was possible to state that no weld failures occurred as a result of only shear stresses in the weld, although two specimens showed evidence of shear mode fracture when a crack, propagated under bending stresses, had reached an appreciable size. Thus, since all the failures were effectively due to bending, rather than shear, the results were (not surprisingly) well above the Class W curve.

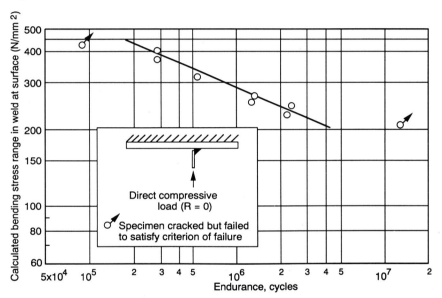

*Figure 6.8    Test results for specimens with single load carrying fillet weld (series PE1), (weld failures initiating at the surface)*

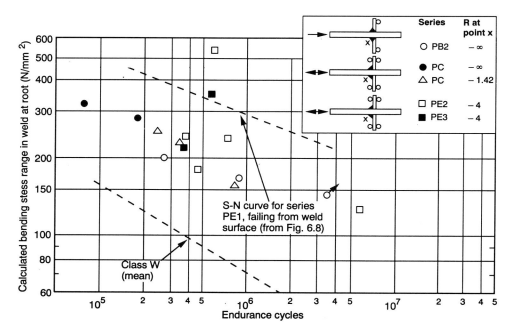

Figure 6.9    Test results for load carrying welds (series PB2 and PC), (weld throat failures initiating at the root)

64

# 7 TROUGH TO CROSS-BEAM CONNECTION

Over the years, several different designs of trough and of trough to cross-beam connections have been employed in orthotropic decks. In the earlier bridges the longitudinal trough stiffeners tended to be trapezoidal in cross-section, typically 3 to 4.5m in length and butted up to the transverse cross-beams. The troughs were then fillet welded all round on both sides of the cross-beam. In the U.K., however, later designs have generally favoured 'V' shaped troughs which have been made in much greater lengths, passing through cut-outs in the cross-beams and being joined, end to end, some distance away from a cross-beam. In addition, a 'cope-hole' has normally been cut in the cross-beam at the apex of the trough. This later design has both fabrication and fatigue advantages. In particular, fit-up between the end of the trough and the cross-beam is no longer critical. A summary of some of the designs which have been used in Britain is shown in Fig. 7.1. The majority of the work considered below was, however, concerned with the early design of trapezoidal trough stiffener fitted between the cross-beams (Fig. 7.1a).

## 7.1 Troughs fitted between cross-beams

In this type of joint three modes of fatigue cracking are possible:

a) through the weld throat from the root;
b) through the trough from the weld toe;
c) in the cross-beam from the weld toe.

It will be recalled that, in the full-scale trial at Denham, the first failures to occur were in some of the trough to cross-beam joints, with cracking being located in the fillet weld connecting the lower 'flange' of the trapezoidal trough to the cross-beam (see Fig. 7.2). At Denham the maximum compressive stress adjacent to that weld was about 85N/mm2 and the corresponding maximum tensile stress was about 9N/mm2.

Thus, since the tensile stress was always very small, it was concluded that the fatigue damage must have been due to the compressive stress ranges caused by the traffic loading. It was also deduced at that time that, for the crack to propagate through the weld as it did, there must have been tensile residual stresses present. In fact, however, several of the residual stress measurements which were made showed the residual stresses in that region to be compressive, albeit at some 40mm from the weld toe, and this created some difficulties in understanding the mechanism of cracking.

Another important factor was whether or not the load was being transmitted from the trough to the cross-beam through the weld metal or by direct bearing through the end of the trough; in other

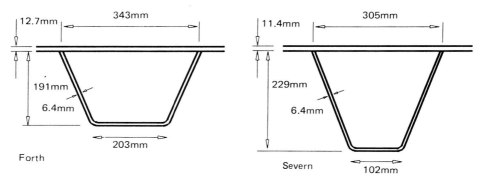

a) Continuous crossbeams with troughs fitted between them Fillet welded all round

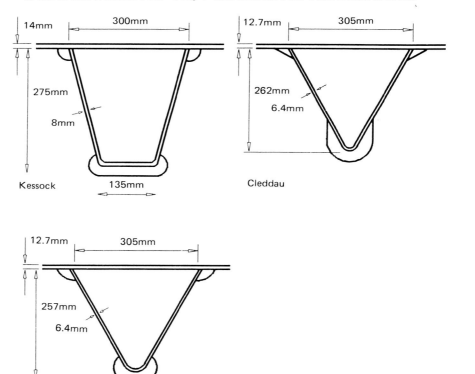

b) Troughs continuous through crossbeam Fillet welded to both sides of crossbeam
(6 – 6.5mm fillets)

*Figure 7.1   Some typical trough to cross-beam connections*

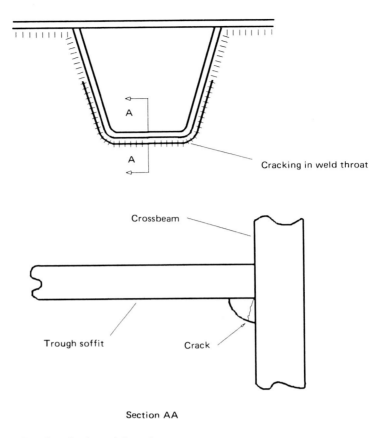

Section AA

*Figure 7.2    Position of cracks in Denham trial panels*

words whether or not there was a gap between the end of the trough and the cross-beam after welding. In the case of the Denham panels the existence of a gap showed that the fillet weld was transmitting the load in shear, but it was hoped that, in the actual bridge, with the joint being jacked together during welding, the gap would be eliminated.

Nevertheless there were serious doubts as to whether that could really be achieved due, for example, to local distortions. An estimate was therefore made, by fracture mechanics (albeit of a rather rudimentary nature), of the size of gap which would just not close under vehicle loading. For a stress of 60N/mm2 in the trough the relevant gap was calculated to be about 0.012mm with a 6mm fillet weld. It was clear that a gap of that size would put such stringent limits on the flatness, both of the surface of the cross-beam web and of the end of the trough, that it was almost inevitable that gaps would exist in service. As a result it was concluded that there was a need to obtain more information on the fatigue behaviour of that type of joint. Clearly it was a joint which was potentially at risk, and in the Severn Crossing, for example, there are some 10,000 such welds under the slow lane and another 10,000 in the offside lane if that were also used by heavy vehicles.

In addition, as discussed in chapter 4, the trough to cross-beam joint happens to be one which appears to derive very little benefit from surfacing and it is also unusual in that influence lines

67

of stress measured around the connections are very long, sufficiently long for front and rear wheels of heavy goods vehicles (HGVs) to interact to give cumulative stresses. This is illustrated in Fig. 7.3 which shows typical influence lines of stress measured close to the weld at the bottom of the trough. The influence line for a single wheel is seen to extend to the next cross-beam. With axle spacings typically of the same order as the cross-beam spacings, interaction of the front and rear wheels produces stresses shown by the dotted line. This effect is compared, in Fig. 7.3(b), with the much shorter influence line associated with the cross-beam to deck plate connection

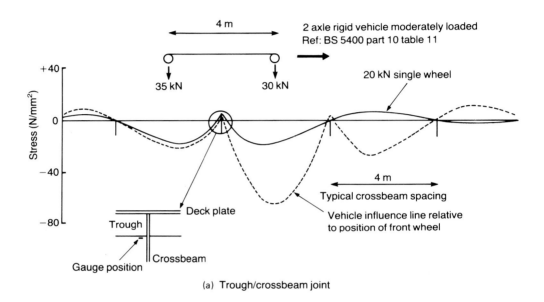

(a) Trough/crossbeam joint

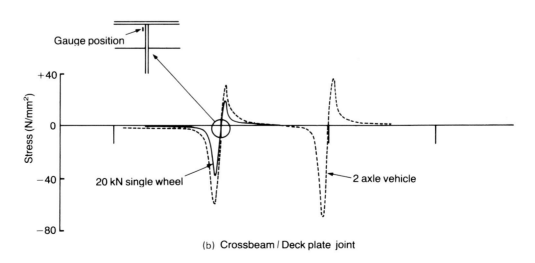

(b) Crossbeam / Deck plate joint

*Figure 7.3 Comparison of single wheel and vehicle influence lines*

68

where interaction does not occur. This latter example is typical of most other welded connections on the deck.

The combination of low weld classification, cumulative stresses under vehicle loading and little beneficial effect from surfacing makes the trough to cross-beam connection a particularly fatigue prone detail. As a result a lengthy fatigue testing programme was put in hand, which not only included tests on specimens simulating the joint in the as-built condition but which also involved a study of several possible repair and strengthening procedures.

For much of the work the specimens consisted of 1500 x 600mm sections of deck plate with a single full-size trapezoidal trough stiffener welded longitudinally at the centre of width and with a web plate at mid-length to represent the cross-beam (Fig. 7.4). This section was intended to be large enough to give a representative stress distribution at the trough to cross-beam connection and to retain the residual stresses induced by welding. To ensure consistency all the specimens were fabricated by the same welder, using manual metal arc welding techniques. An assembly jig was used to hold the components while welding was completed on each side of the cross-beam in turn. In view of the long endurances hoped for, the ends of the specimen were strengthened to prevent premature failure at the loading points.

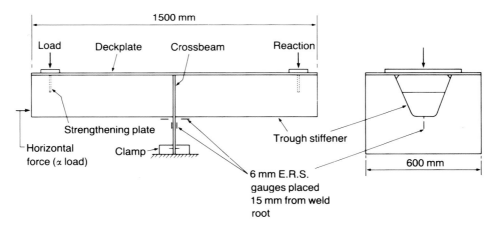

*Figure 7.4    Typical specimen used to represent the trough to cross-beam joint*

A novel loading arrangement (Fig. 7.5) was used which was designed to reproduce the in-service stress distribution at the joint. It involved having the test section supported on the cross-beam (which was clamped to a fixed base) and loaded in three-point bending by a servo-hydraulic actuator at one end with a reaction point at the other end. This arrangement generated compressive longitudinal stress in the soffit of the trough and compressive axial stress in the cross-beam. The required bending stress in the cross-beam (range 80-100% of the stress range in the trough) was induced by the linkage device shown in Fig. 7.5. A connecting link between the test rig base and the end of the specimen, at an angle of 30° to the horizontal, caused the end of the specimen to move in an arc, rather than vertically, under an applied load. The resulting horizontal displacement induced bending stresses in the restrained cross-beam, which could be considered proportional to the applied load over the small distances involved. To avoid changes in displacement during a long test due to mechanical wear, it was necessary to design the device

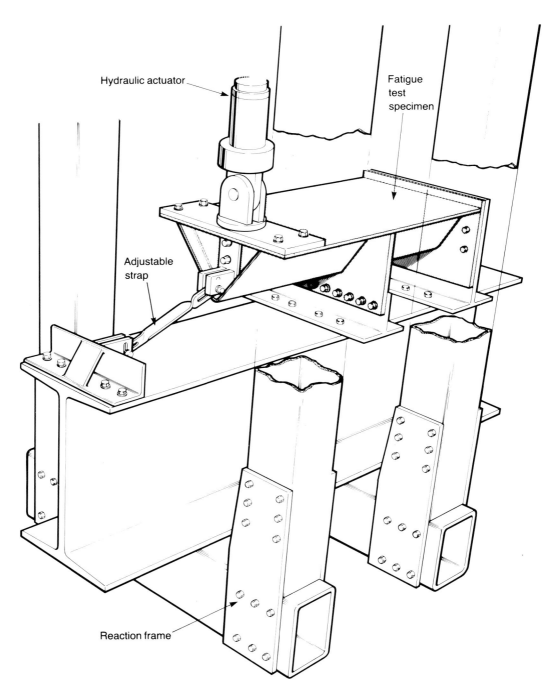

Figure 7.5    Arrangement of test rig for fatigue tests on single stiffener specimens (note: the figure shows a V
section trough, but the same arrangement was used for tests on trapezoidal troughs)

70

with no moving parts. Thus the cross-section of the link was chosen to have minimal resistance to bending in the vertical plane, while retaining adequate axial strength.

In addition to the tests on relatively small specimens, outlined above, some tests were also carried out on full-size deck panels, measuring 14 x 3.7m, details of which are shown in Fig. 7.6. The spacing of the cross-beams was reduced at each end in order to represent longitudinal continuity, while transverse continuity was represented by channel sections on the edges of the panel. The panels were supported (see Fig. 7.7) by inverted Tee sections welded to the cross-beams, with the Tee sections supported on stiff I section beams.

The panel was loaded by means of two servo-hydraulic actuators, positioned either side of the cross-beam, through two 25mm thick rubber loading pads. These were included to represent the contact patch of a tyre. By applying the actuator loads out of phase it was possible to simulate the passage of a single wheel along the trough centreline. Thus, for each 'axle passage', there was one load application by each actuator giving two (compressive) stress cycles in the trough and one, nominally alternating ($R = -1$), cycle in the cross-beam. In contrast, the loading on the small specimens was restricted to one actuator which produced, for each load cycle, one stress cycle in the trough and one, concurrently, in the cross-beam. A comparison between these two types of loading is shown in Fig. 7.8.

The results obtained for the 'as-fabricated' specimens, made with 6mm fillet welds, are shown in Fig. 7.9. This includes results both from small specimen and from panel tests. Except for the panel specimen indicated, the mode of failure in all these specimens was essentially the same as that which occurred in the Denham trial, with cracking being initiated at the weld root, mostly on the web of the trough (typically about 35mm up from the soffit), and propagating in the fillet weld between the trough and the cross-beam. In the 'odd' panel specimen cracking was located at the weld toe in the cross-beam.

The fact that the cracks were situated adjacent to the trough web rather than in the more highly stressed region adjacent to the soffit was interesting and was found to be related to the residual stress distribution. Cracking in the weld on the web occurred in joints where the weld across the soffit was made first, followed by the web welds. If the welding sequence was reversed, thus reversing the pattern of the residual stresses, cracking occurred in the soffit weld. Both types of crack have been observed on a bridge, consistent with the sequence of welding. Cracks in the web were from the weld root, but soffit cracks tended to be at the toe on the cross-beam. These are, incidentally, more difficult to repair.

In order to simplify later comparisons, all the results in Fig. 7.9 are expressed in terms of the longitudinal stress range in the soffit of the trough, as measured by 6mm strain gauges situated 15mm from the weld root. Effectively, therefore, the gauges should have been outside the region of stress concentration, so that the quoted stresses can be assumed to be 'nominal' values. It will be noted that there was excellent agreement between the results obtained with the small specimens and with the panels, the lower limit of the scatter band being virtually coincident with the mean -2 standard deviations design curve for Class F in BS 5400. Thus, given that the results relate to weld throat failure rather than toe failure, this suggests that toe failure in the trough can be regarded as corresponding, at a minimum, to Class F.

Some comparable results obtained using the small specimens, but loaded in three-point bending

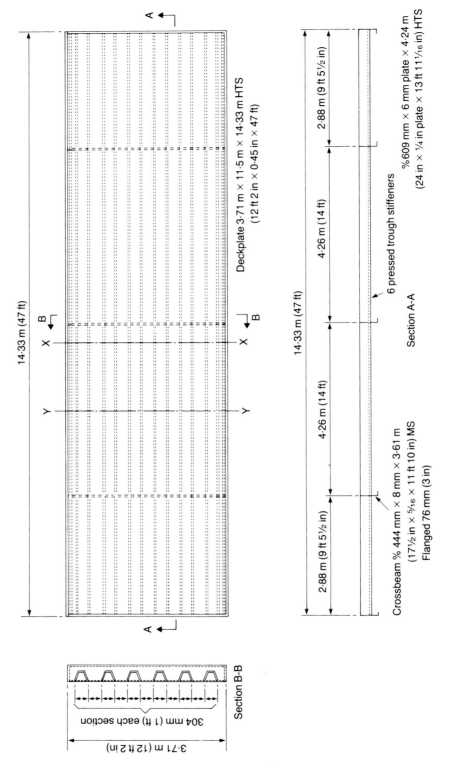

14·33 m (47 ft)

Deckplate 3·71 m × 11·5 m × 14·33 m HTS
(12 ft 2 in × 0·45 in × 47 ft)

3·71 m (12 ft 2 in)

304 mm (1 ft) each section

Section B-B

14·33 m (47 ft)

2·88 m (9 ft 5½ in)

4·26 m (14 ft)

4·26 m (14 ft)

2·88 m (9 ft 5½ in)

6 pressed trough stiffeners

%609 mm × 6 mm plate × 4·24 m
(24 in × ¼ in plate × 13 ft 11¹¹⁄₁₆ in) HTS

Crossbeam % 444 mm × 8 mm × 3·61 m
(17½ in × ⁵⁄₁₆ × 11 ft 10 in) MS
Flanged 76 mm (3 in)

Section A-A

Note:
All material noted HTS high tensile steel to BS 968 (1962)
All material noted MS mild steel to BS 15

*Figure 7.6    Deck panel used for static and fatigue tests*

72

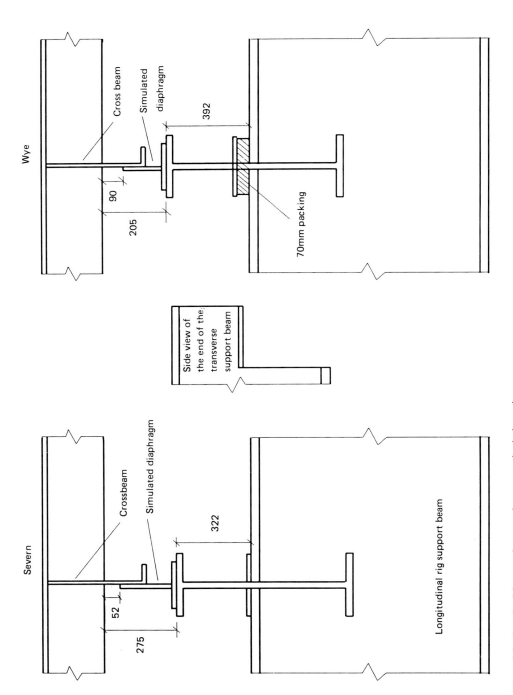

Wye

Cross beam

Simulated diaphragm

392

90

205

70mm packing

Side view of
the end of the
transverse
support beam

Severn

Crossbeam

Simulated diaphragm

322

52

275

Longitudinal rig support beam

73

*Figure 7.7    Details of the cross-beam used to support the deck panel*

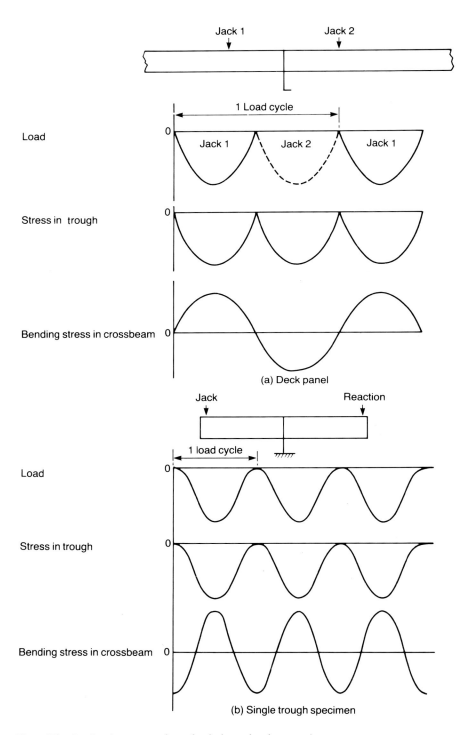

*Figure 7.8   Load and stress waveforms for deck panel and test specimen*

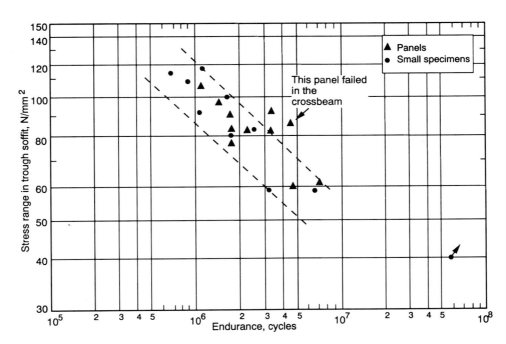

*Figure 7.9    Test results for as-built trough to cross-beam joints, with 6mm fillet welds failing in the weld throat*

such that there was no load, axial or bending, in the 'cross-beam', are shown in Fig. 7.10. In these tests a comparison was made between the strengths of specimens with and without a gap between the end of the trough and the 'cross-beam', and results were obtained for three stress ratios, with the stress in the soffit of the trough subjected to tensile or compressive loading (both at R = 0) and also to alternating loading (R = -1). All the specimens failed in the weld from the weld root, mainly on the trough web.

To some extent the results were 'odd', in that the specimens with gaps consistently gave longer lives than the specimens without gaps, although that is a reflection of the fact that the load required to produce the same stress range was lower for the specimens with a gap (35kN) than for those without a gap (45kN). It seems probable that this apparent anomaly was due to the creation of more local bending in the trough soffit when a gap was present.

Clearly the results for the specimens without gaps were significantly lower than those obtained earlier (Fig. 7.9) and their strength in terms of the stress range in the trough soffit was equivalent to Class G in BS 5400. Thus, taking account of the fact that the stress at the actual point of failure initiation (on the web) was obviously lower than at the soffit, but that with a different residual stress distribution failure might occur at the soffit, it seems reasonable for the fillet weld itself to be designed to Class W. However, this implies that it would probably not be possible to utilise the full Class F design stress in the trough adjacent to the end connection since the weld would be too big in relation to the flange thickness.

In the light of these results it was clear that there was little chance of this particular joint surviving with no failures for the full desired life of the structure, namely 120 years. In fact the first cracking of trough to cross-beam joints in the Severn Crossing was noticed in 1977 (i.e. after just over 10

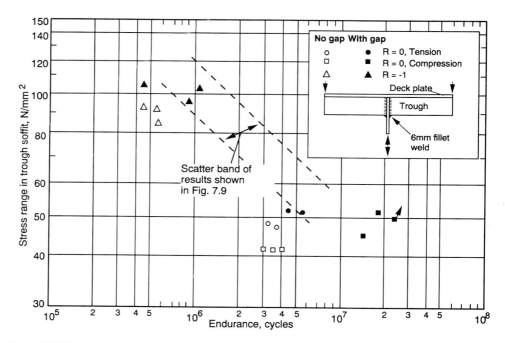

*Figure 7.10  Test results for trough to cross-beam joint, with and without a gap between trough and cross-beam, failing in the weld*

years). As a result, a large number of possible methods for either improving the fatigue life of the joint, or for repairing the weld when cracking did occur, were considered and several were investigated experimentally. In generic terms, however, they can be divided into three main categories:

1)   overwelding and rewelding.
2)   inducing a favourable residual stress system.
3)   strengthening the joint with various forms of brackets.

It is convenient to consider separately the work on each of these categories of repair.

### 7.1.1  Overwelding and rewelding

Regardless of the other possibilities, summarised below, it was obvious that the simplest repair option would be to grind out the cracked weld and reinstate it with another of the same size (i.e. a 6mm leg length fillet weld). Clearly this would only be a practical option provided that the number of failures occurring at any one time remained reasonable. The implication of following this course of action was that, since the repair would, presumably, have the same fatigue life (assuming no change in loading) as the original weld, the worst affected joints might have to be replaced about 20 times in order to achieve the required 120 year life. At the same time it raised the question of whether or not the fatigue strength of a repeatedly repaired joint remained constant, regardless of the number of times it was repaired.

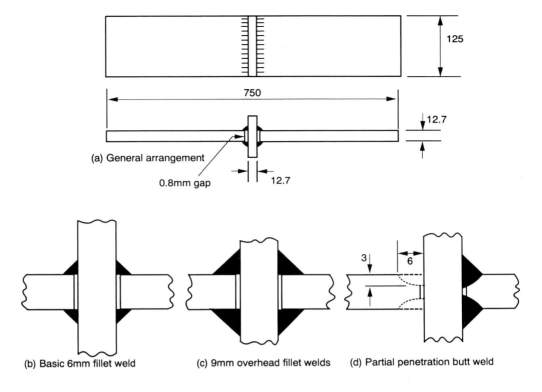

Figure 7.11 Plate specimens used to represent the trough to cross-beam joint

However, since the failures in the original design of the connection were all in the weld throat, there were two other obvious possibilities to be considered. The first was to increase the size of the fillet weld by rewelding after first grinding out the existing, cracked, weld. The second was to replace the fillet weld with a partial penetration butt weld, which would certainly be expected to give a higher fatigue strength, but with the disadvantage of increased fabrication costs.

Each of these possible repair methods was evaluated both by tests on trough specimens and also by tests using a simplified and idealised form of specimen, the latter being both cheaper and quicker. Details of the simple plate specimens are shown in Fig. 7.11. They consisted essentially of two plates, 12.7mm thick, representing the bottom flanges of the troughs, with a central transverse plate representing the web of the cross-girder. The gap between them was nominally 0.8mm wide. It will be noted that the main plates of the specimens were twice the thickness of the actual troughs and that the specimens had welds on both plate surfaces, whereas the trough is only welded to the diaphragm around its outer surface. Thus the specimens can be regarded as simulating two joints back to back.

The objective of this design was to have a symmetrical specimen which could be loaded axially in a standard testing machine. Although it was not an ideal simulation of the joint which exists in service, it was felt that it would be suitable for providing comparative data on the three joint designs. By using a symmetrical specimen bending transverse to the plane of the plate was, of course, eliminated, but at the time it seemed likely that there would in any case be little bending in the bottom flange of the trough owing to the stiffening effect of the trough webs.

Details of the three types of joint which were tested are also shown in Fig. 7.11. The first series simulated the existing joint and had 6mm fillet welds made in one run in the flat position. In the other two series, however, the welds were made overhead so as to simulate the type of weld which could be made on the bridge. The second series had a simple fillet weld with the leg length increased to (nominally) 9.5mm, which was made in three runs. In the third series the ends of the (trough) plates were prepared, by air arc gouging overhead, in order to try to obtain a partial penetration butt weld. The depth of the gouge was 3mm and the width on the surface 6mm. The welds were then made in three runs.

In the particular specimens which were used it would have been possible to obtain a full penetration weld, since welding was carried out from both sides. In the actual bridge, however, it was considered that it would almost certainly be necessary to avoid burning through the trough if a satisfactory weld were to be made, so that there would exist an area of partial lack of penetration in the weld root. In the specimens this was simulated by having a lack of penetration 'defect' approximately 3mm deep at the centre of plate thickness. Typical shapes of the various welds are shown in Fig. 7.12.

The specimens were tested under axial compressive loading at $R = 0$ and the results are summarised in Fig. 7.13. All the specimens with 6mm fillet welds duly failed through the weld throat, as in the Denham trial panels, with a strength at $2 \times 10^6$ cycles of about 60N/mm2 (based on plate cross-section). As can be seen from Fig. 7.13, the relevant S-N curve is slightly below the lower limit of the scatter band for single trough specimens. Nevertheless, these simple specimens did appear to be a reasonable simulation of the actual joint, but it is interesting to note that, in terms of weld throat shear stress, the strength at $2 \times 10^6$ cycles was about 86N/mm2; this is far above the strength specified for Class W (57N/mm2 mean stress).

For the other two series the results were more scattered but the strength was clearly improved. For the 9mm fillet welds the lower limit strength was increased to about 130N/mm2 (in the plate) at $2 \times 10^6$ cycles, which is equivalent to about 126N/mm2 weld throat shear stress, while for the partial penetration butt welds there was a clear tendency to obtain a still higher strength, although the lower limit was approximately the same. In these two series, also, the majority of the specimens failed through the weld throat, but a significant number, indicated in Fig. 7.13, also had cracks at the weld toe. This suggests that, in the conventional sense, those specimens had welds of close to optimum size, the optimum design corresponding to an equal chance of failure from the toe or through the weld throat. In this particular application, however, a joint design which resulted in failure in the trough from the weld toe would be much more expensive to repair than one giving throat failure, so that the definition of 'optimum' is rather different.

Nevertheless, it was considered sensible to check the results obtained with these simple specimens by testing some single trough specimens repaired with 9mm fillet and partial penetration welds. Considering first those with 9mm fillet welds, the welding was carried out in the overhead position, in order to simulate site conditions, and the welding sequence was devised to prevent relative movement of the trough and cross-beam, in order to cope with the situation on a structure under traffic. This involved first cutting out and remaking the welds on the trough web and then the weld on the trough soffit. The results which were obtained (Fig. 7.14) show that, in contrast to those obtained with the simple specimens, the use of a larger fillet weld did not lead to any increase in strength although the mode of failure was different; in these larger specimens fatigue cracks formed at the weld toe in the cross-beam adjacent to the trough soffit.

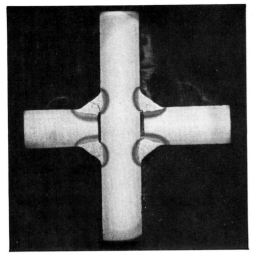

a. Simple 1/4 in fillet weld made downhand

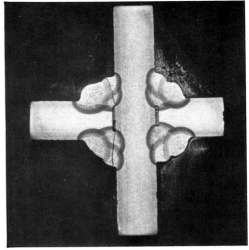

b. 3/8 in g length weld made overhead

I 10mm

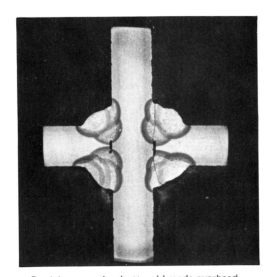

c. Partial penetration butt weld made overhead

*Figure 7.12  Macrosections showing typical weld shapes and modes of failure*

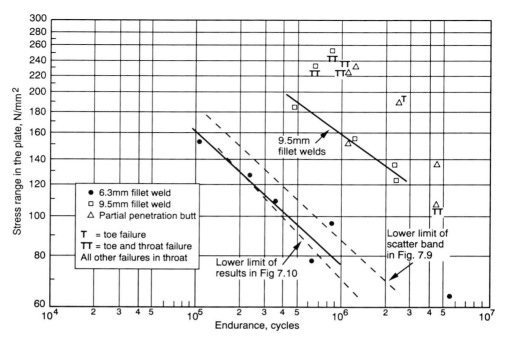

*Figure 7.13 Test results for transverse load-carrying fillet welded specimens (fig 7.11) subjected to axial compressive loading*

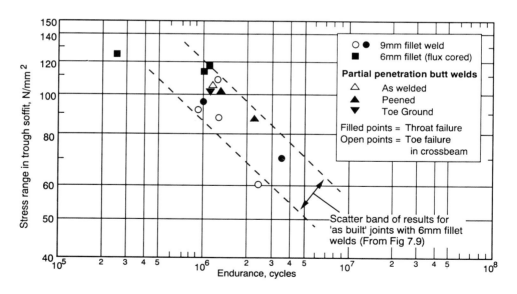

*Figure 7.14 Test results for trough to cross-beam joints repaired by rewelding*

In two further specimens, welded in the reverse order (i.e. the soffit weld before the web welds), failure occurred in the same manner as in the original joints, with cracking in the weld throat. This tends to confirm the view that the mode of failure is largely determined by the residual stress distribution, which in turn depends upon the weld sequence. It appears to be largely the differences in residual stress which prevented the improvement predicted by the small-scale tests being realised.

In spite of these difficulties, it is at least possible that a higher strength might have been obtained with a still larger weld, although it would have necessitated the use of weld toe treatment (e.g. by toe grinding) to increase the fatigue strength of the joint failing from the toe. On the other hand, to make such welds would require more weld runs. The next size increase would probably involve a weld made with six runs instead of three, so that there is also a need to balance strength requirements against economic considerations.

Turning now to the repairs made with a partial penetration butt weld it is worth noting that this repair procedure necessarily involves considerable practical difficulties, not only in preparing the end of the longitudinal trough but also in rewelding. As far as weld preparation is concerned, owing to limited access and variations in trough dimensions, considerable development would be required to devise an economic method of machining. Arc-air gouging is not attractive because of the difficulty of maintaining an adequate tolerance, and the risk of damage to the surrounding steelwork. Similarly, the difficulties of welding follow from the geometry of the connection. Access is only to one side of the joint and a backing strip cannot be provided. Added to the normal difficulties of overhead site welding it seemed unlikely that it would be possible to achieve and maintain a consistent standard of welding and reasonable freedom from defects. In any case it was clear that such welds would be more expensive than fillet welds, because of the extra cost of joint preparation and the additional welding required to fill the penetration. In fact the fatigue test results, also included in Fig. 7.14, again showed that the strength was no greater than the original fillet welded connection, so no further effort was made to solve the welding problems. In these specimens the majority of the failures were in the weld throat of the soffit weld, the weld toe on the cross-beam having been treated either by toe grinding or by hammer peening. The specimen which was not treated still failed from the weld toe in the cross-beam.

Finally, in the light of limited evidence that welds made with flux-cored electrodes tended to give a superior fatigue performance to those made by normal manual metal arc welding, three tests were carried out on single trough specimens repaired by that method. The results, again included in Fig. 7.14, show that two of the specimens gave lives which were very similar to that of the as-built connection, while the third was unexpectedly short. Clearly, however, this approach did not give an enhanced fatigue strength.

### 7.1.2 Residual stress methods

In many types of welded joint, particularly those involving failure from the weld toe, it is often possible to obtain very large increases in fatigue strength by the application of various techniques to produce high compressive residual stresses at the point of expected crack initiation. They include, for example, hammer or shot peening, spot heating, local compression and overloading, among others. Few of these are even mentioned in most design Standards, although all have been used on occasions; nevertheless peening is by far the most commonly used technique.

In this particular instance, however, the mode of failure involved cracking initiating at the root of the trough to cross-girder fillet weld rather than at the weld toe. Thus the only possible method of introducing compressive residual stresses appeared to be to overload the connection in some way so that the weld root would be in tension during the overload and hence be subjected to compressive residual stresses after unloading.

There were, however, two obvious difficulties with this approach. The first was that it would not be possible to measure the residual stress at the weld root, so that it would not be possible to check whether or not compressive residual stresses had in fact been induced at the root. The second was of a practical nature, in that the load would have to be applied in such a way as to generate tensile stresses in the soffit of the trough adjacent to the weld and this could only be achieved by jacking upwards on the trough, which would certainly require strengthening of the trough soffit and a suitable reaction point. In view of these difficulties this possible method of treatment was not considered any further.

### 7.1.3 Strengthening the joint with brackets

During the course of the investigation several different forms of bracket were considered for use in strengthening the longitudinal trough to cross-girder joint. It is convenient to consider each in turn.

#### 7.1.3.1    Stiffening with a flat plate

The first idea was to pass a flat plate through a cut-out in the cross-beam and weld it to the soffit of the troughs on either side of the cross-beam. However, it was found that, in many instances, the troughs on either side of the cross-beam were not in line. In addition, it was considered that, in effect, this would merely involve transferring the point of weakness from the weld between the trough and cross-girder to that between the trough and strap with no reduction in stress or improvement in fatigue strength of the detail. It was therefore anticipated that this would give no improvement in strength and no further work was carried out on it.

#### 7.1.3.2    The addition of gusset plates

One method of reducing the stress in the trough to cross-beam weld was to weld triangular brackets in the corner between the two. Initially two specimens were made which each had 12mm thick gussets welded to the soffit of the trough on each side of the cross-beam, the ends of the welds on the trough being ground to reduce the stress concentration. Unfortunately, however, failure still occurred at the ends of the gussets in the trough at lives less than that of the as-built joint.

Subsequently the idea was re-examined but with the gussets increased in number, reduced in thickness to 5mm and shaped to reduce the stress concentration at their ends (Fig. 7.15). In addition the gussets were repositioned on the web of the trough rather than on its soffit and the weld toes at both ends of the gusset were hammer peened, as was the toe of the fillet weld between

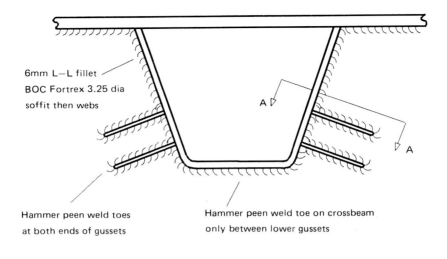

6mm L—L fillet
BOC Fortrex 3.25 dia
soffit then webs

A

A

Hammer peen weld toes
at both ends of gussets

Hammer peen weld toe on crossbeam
only between lower gussets

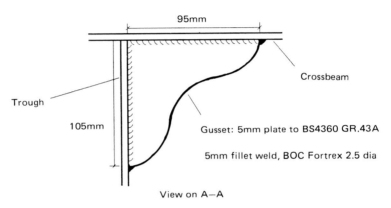

95mm

Crossbeam

Trough

105mm

Gusset: 5mm plate to BS4360 GR.43A

5mm fillet weld, BOC Fortrex 2.5 dia

View on A—A

*Figure 7.15  Welded gusset repair for trough to cross-beam joint*

the trough and the cross-beam on the cross-beam. These measures were effective in preventing failure from the weld toes, cracking now occurring in the throats of the trough to cross-beam and the trough to gusset welds. Although the test results obtained from three single trough specimens (see Fig. 7.16) were quite encouraging, a similar joint on a deck panel gave a considerably lower strength, near the upper end of the scatter band for 'as-built' joints with 6mm fillet welds.

An alternative method of adding gussets, which was tested on two specimens, was to bond them with a structural hot cure single part epoxy adhesive. Installation was complicated by the need to heat the joint without using a direct flame, and because the adhesive became a thin liquid at the cure temperatures (120°C) and had to be sealed in place. However, the results were not particularly successful, since the gussets debonded from the cross-beam under dynamic loading, thereby effectively removing the strengthening.

83

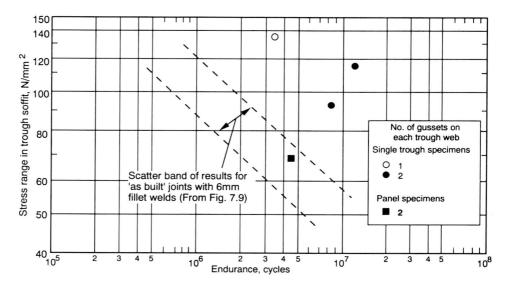

*Figure 7.16  Test results for trough to cross-beam joint strengthened with welded gussets*

### 7.1.3.3 Welded strap on the trough

The origin of the idea to use a welded strap around the trough was to try to circumvent the problems of making the preparation for a butt welded trough to cross-beam connection. It involved removing the existing weld and then welding a strap over the end of the trough, generally as indicated in Fig. 7.17.

The initial trials involved the use of a preformed strap, 8mm x 75mm. The end adjacent to the cross-beam was prepared before assembly and the strap was then butt welded to the cross-beam and fillet welded to the trough.

At about that time, however, it was becoming apparent that a butt weld did not seem to give any significant improvement over a fillet weld, so the strap was reduced in size to 8 x 40mm and was attached by 6mm fillet welds. In addition it became apparent that relatively small variations in the size of the troughs would cause installation difficulties on site if preformed straps were used. Hence, following the achievement of encouraging results in the early tests, a technique was developed to enable the straps to be formed in situ, and to fit closely around troughs of varying cross-section.

The main features of the device are shown in Fig. 7.18. The installation procedure is to wedge the strap in position under the soffit of the trough, then heat and bend it round the trough corners to fit closely to the webs of the trough. The strap is then tack welded in position, the wedges removed and welding completed following the specified sequence. The weld toes on the cross-beam and on the trough are then hammer peened to prevent failure through the plate.

The decision to employ hammer peening resulted from the fact that the first specimen to be tested failed from the weld toe in the cross-beam at a life which was only marginally superior to that for the as-built joints (Fig. 7.19). After peening, however, all except one of the single trough specimens gave failure in the weld throat, mainly in the strap to cross-girder weld but occasionally in the strap to trough weld, at lives which represented a substantial improvement

84

over that for the as-built joints. The single specimen which did not fail in a weld throat failed from the toe of the strap to cross-girder weld in the strap, but again at a greatly improved life.

In view of the predominant mode of failure, an attempt was made to increase the strength of the joint by increasing the strap thickness from 8 to 10mm, in order to enable a larger fillet weld to be made at the strap to trough junction. At the same time the other end of the strap was prepared to allow a penetration weld to be made between the strap and the cross-girder. However, as can be seen from Fig. 7.19, these modifications produced no improvement in fatigue strength.

Nevertheless the results obtained using the welded strap repair on single trough specimens were, in general, very encouraging and it was therefore decided to carry out some additional tests on the panel specimens. Those results are also included in Fig. 7.19. Except for one specimen, which failed from the toe of the strap to cross-beam weld in the strap, all the failures were in the throat of that weld. As can be seen from Fig. 7.19, the lives which were obtained were generally lower than those for the single trough specimens but they were still a considerable improvement on those for the 'as-built' joint.

*7.1.3.4      The addition of bolted brackets*
The idea behind the possible use of a high strength friction grip (HSFG) bolted connection was that such joints tend to be less prone to fatigue than welded joints. On the other hand it was recognised that the installation of a bolted connection would be more difficult, time-consuming and costly than rewelding and that it would add to the dead-weight of the structure; the need to accommodate fabrication tolerances in the troughs would reduce the efficiency of the connection in this respect. A further problem was that, because of the difficulty of access to the inside of the trough, the connection would have to be a single lap joint, which might give rise to fatigue problems due to local bending stresses.

The first design considered was a combination joint consisting of HSFG bolted brackets used to strengthen a rewelded connection. To achieve the twenty-fold improvement in fatigue life, which was considered to be necessary at that time, it was apparent that the stress range would have to be reduced by 65%, i.e. the bolted part of the combination would have to carry 65% of the applied load. Few data are available on the fatigue performance of combination joints but in view of the limited deformation capacity of welded joints it would be difficult to devise a bolted connection with sufficient stiffness to carry a major part of the load. Also a combination would seem to have all the disadvantages of a bolted connection without eliminating the problems associated with welding. As a result it was decided to design a joint in which the weld was replaced by a bolted joint.

In principle it was decided that the repair should involve two pairs of brackets fitted to the trough webs on either side of the cross-beam (Fig. 7.20). This configuration was chosen in preference to a single pair of brackets on the soffit of the trough because of the risk of failure in the cross-beam. Angle brackets were selected in preference to plates passing through the cross-beam so that misalignment of the troughs could be tolerated. The method of assembly was to fit the brackets to the trough web with the aid of an access hole in the soffit before drilling through the cross-beam and bracket flanges. This enabled assembly of the bolts even if the brackets on opposite sides of the cross-beam were not in line. To preserve the static strength of the trough the

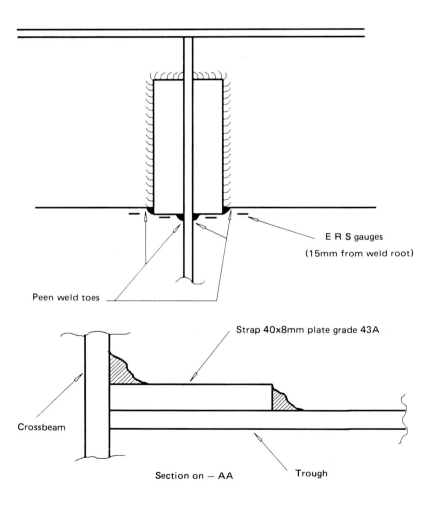

E R S gauges
(15mm from weld root)

Peen weld toes

Strap 40x8mm plate grade 43A

Crossbeam

Section on — AA

Trough

*Figure 7.17  Details of welded strap repair for trough to cross-beam joint*

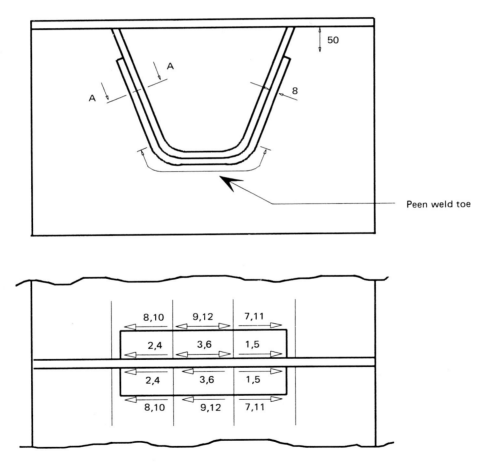

50

A

A

8

Peen weld toe

| 8,10 | 9,12 | 7,11 |
| 2,4 | 3,6 | 1,5 |
| 2,4 | 3,6 | 1,5 |
| 8,10 | 9,12 | 7,11 |

Strap weld sequence

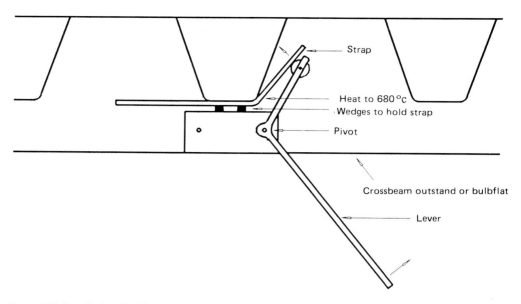

*Figure 7.18 Installation of welded strap*

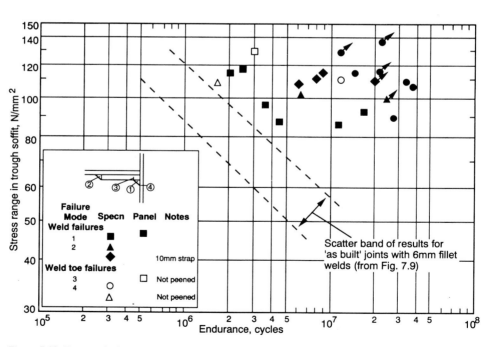

*Figure 7.19 Test results for trough to cross-beam joint repaired with welded straps*

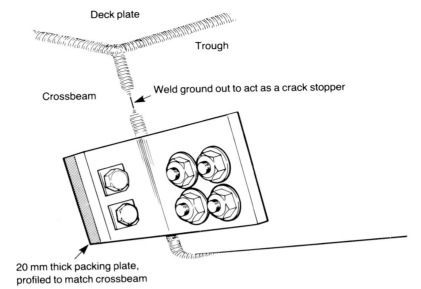

Deck plate

Trough

Crossbeam

Weld ground out to act as a crack stopper

20 mm thick packing plate,
profiled to match crossbeam

(a) View from side

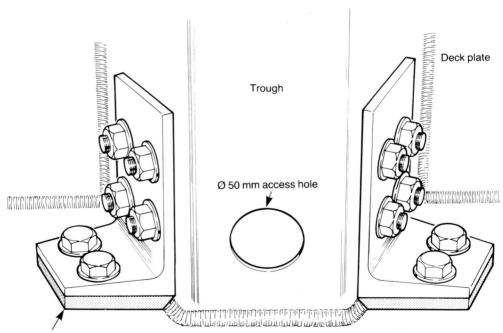

Trough

Deck plate

Ø 50 mm access hole

Trough 20 mm thick packing plate,
profiled to match crossbeam

(b) View from underneath

*Figure 7.20  Trough to cross-beam joint with bolted bracket repair*

89

50mm diameter access hole was close to the cross-beam at a point where the load normally carried by the soffit had been transferred to the angle brackets.

In some of the early trials the brackets were fabricated from rolled angle sections but, as discussed below, this tended to lead to fatigue failure in the brackets initiating at the root radius. In general, therefore, the brackets were fabricated from split 381 x 102mm channel section in order to obtain the benefits of a larger root radius and a thicker flange than was available in a rolled angle section.

In the first specimen to be tested, with the brackets fabricated from 381 x 102mm channel section and with the welds omitted, the joint was unbroken after 33 x 10⁶ cycles at a stress range of 90N/mm2 (see Fig. 7.21). As a result it was decided to try to reduce the weight penalty by using brackets formed from 9.5 or 12.7mm thick rolled angle sections. The result, however, was for failures to occur either in the brackets, initiating at the corner radius, or in the cross-beam at the toe of the trough to cross-beam weld. (At this stage this was effectively a non-load-carrying fillet weld on the cross-beam since the trough had been cut through so as to release it from the weld when the bolted brackets were installed.) As far as the bracket failures were concerned it was noted that the presence of a gap between the bracket flange and the cross-beam could lead to early fatigue failure, so that it was necessary to introduce machined packing pieces to achieve a close fit

As a result the use of angle section brackets was abandoned in favour of brackets formed from a channel section in order to obtain the benefits of a larger root radius and a thicker flange; in addition, the weld toes were shot peened. With these alterations all the first three specimens to be tested reached lives exceeding 25 x 10⁶ cycles at a nominal range in the trough soffit of

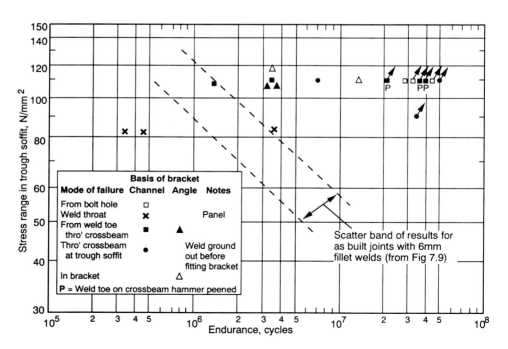

Figure 7.21 Test results for trough to cross-beam joint repaired with bolted brackets

106N/mm2, and in the only specimen to fail cracking initiated from one of the bolt holes in the bracket flange connected to the cross-beam, this hole having become elongated during manufacture because of an alignment problem; the failure occurred, however, at well beyond the required life.

In the light of these encouraging results some further tests were carried out both on single trough specimens and on the full-scale deck panel and the results are included in Fig. 7.21. Unfortunately, it was found that, when tested on a full sized deck panel, the bolted bracket repair was not successful. However, in any case, it was found in the course of installation trials that this was much more difficult and time consuming than the welded repair methods.

## 7.2    Troughs passing through the cross-beams

In this more recent type of joint (Fig. 7.1(b)) the weld between the trough and the cross-beam is no longer 'load-carrying', at least to nothing like the same extent, since the load in the trough is effectively transmitted through the cross-beam into the trough in the next bay. With this approach, therefore, the most likely modes of fatigue cracking are (Fig. 7.22):

a)    in the trough starting from the weld toe;
b)    longitudinally in the trough starting from the weld end adjacent to a cope hole;
c)    in the cross-beam from the same weld ends.

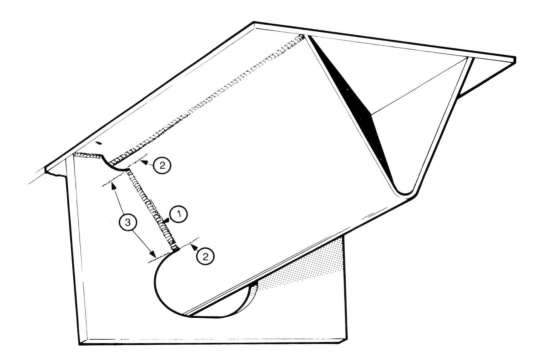

Figure 7.22  Potential modes of failure in trough to cross-beam joints with continuous troughs through the cross-beams

91

As is evident from Fig. 7.1(b) numerous detail designs of the joint are possible and at the start of this particular part of the work a panel was constructed with five V-shaped troughs, the three central connections being of the forms shown in Fig. 7.23. Connections of types A and C are typical of those which have been used in later UK bridges, while Type B, with no cope holes or cut-outs around the trough apex, is commonly used abroad. The panel was then used to determine stresses around the three types of connection under loading applied through a single wheel.

A provisional fatigue assessment was then carried out using the BS 5400 vehicle loading spectrum and assuming that the relevant S-N curve was that for Class F in BS 5400. This showed that the Type B connection had the lowest predicted life and the Type A connection the highest. These were the two joints which were therefore selected for the fatigue testing programme, the method of test being similar to that indicated in Fig. 7.5.

In the Type B specimens cracks initiated, as expected, at the weld toe at the apex of the trough and the results in Fig. 7.24 are presented in terms of the stress at the trough apex measured 15mm from the weld root. The lives relate to a crack length of 25mm. It will be seen from Fig. 7.24 that the results correspond closely to the Class E mean S-N curve in BS 5400 and this seems to be a reasonable classification for that joint. The fact that it is a higher classification than for transverse non-load-carrying fillet welds in BS 5400 (Class F) is not inconsistent with an expected beneficial 'thickness effect' resulting from the fact that the trough was only 6mm thick.

In the case of the Type A connection all three of the expected modes of failure, listed above, were encountered. Considering first the failures along the weld toe in the trough, the results are again included in Fig. 7.24, but in this case the relevant stress is that measured 15mm from the weld root and 10mm above the weld end (see sketch in Fig. 7.24). Rather surprisingly, the fatigue strength was very much higher, albeit with one low result. However, even that result was above the mean - 2 standard deviations design curve for Class C.

In general, however, this type of cracking only occurred after the formation of cracks running longitudinally in the trough and starting in the cope hole from the upper end of the fillet weld on the trough web. The relevant results, plotted in terms of the stress measured 15mm from the weld end, are shown in Fig. 7.25, and it can be seen that they are equivalent to Class G in BS 5400. Clearly this is, therefore, a low strength joint and even though, being close to the deck plate, it would probably be improved substantially in strength by the presence of surfacing, the results suggest that it would be beneficial to omit the cope hole around the trough to deck plate welds. On the other hand, they also suggest that an optimised design would still incorporate the cut-out in the cross-beam around the trough apex. However, further testing would be needed to assess the design. In particular, the following points would need to be investigated:

1.  The fatigue strength in relation to cracks initiating at the top of the trough where the three welds (trough to deck plate, cross-beam to deck plate, and trough to cross-beam) meet. This is not a good design detail. Cracks did not develop there during the fatigue tests on the Type B specimens but the loading was not arranged to produce highest stresses at that point.

2.  The possibility of cracks initiating at the weld end, through the trough plate, at the bottom of the weld. Cracks did not occur there in the tests on the Type A specimens but, again, the loading was not arranged to produce highest stresses at that point. A poor classification

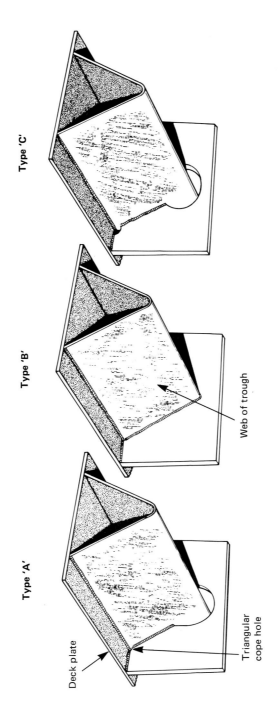

Type 'A'

Type 'B'

Type 'C'

Deck plate

Triangular
cope hole

Web of trough

*Figure 7.23 Types of connection between continuous troughs and cross-beam*

93

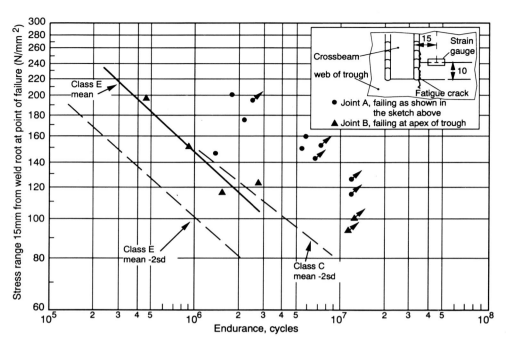

*Figure 7.24 Test results for through trough to cross-beam joints failing in the trough at the weld toe*

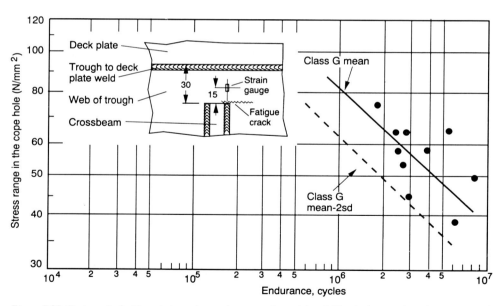

*Figure 7.25 Test results for Type A through trough to cross-beam joints failing in the trough at the upper cope hole*

94

was obtained for the weld end failure at the top of the weld. If a similar classification were obtained at the bottom of the weld, it could become the critical fatigue point.

Finally, as far as fatigue cracking in the cross-beam is concerned, cracks did occur in some specimens at one or more of the weld ends on the trough web. However, these cracks only formed at high stresses and the results represent a high joint classification.


## 7.3    Joint classification

In the light of the results set out in this Chapter, it is clear that there are considerable differences between the fatigue strengths of joints relating to 'fitted' and 'through' troughs. It is therefore convenient to consider them separately.


### 7.3.1  Fitted troughs

As far as the unstiffened joints are concerned, it will be seen from Figs 7.9, 7.10, 7.13 and 7.14 that the great majority of tests gave failure in the weld, even in those situations where the end of the trough was nominally in contact with the cross-beam and the soffit of the trough was under compression loading. It is also apparent (see Figs 7.10 and 7.13, for example) that there was a considerable degree of scatter between the various results.

Unfortunately, the situation is still further complicated by the fact that the cracks in most of the trough to cross-beam specimens were not located at the point of maximum stress (i.e. adjacent to the trough soffit), but at some point on the web, due primarily to the influence of residual stresses. In these circumstances it has proved impossible to reconcile the results in the form of a single S-N curve relating to shear stress in the weld metal, although it seems clear that such a strength would certainly be better than that defined by Class W in BS 5400.

In view of this situation it seems more appropriate to classify the joint in relation to the stress in the trough soffit rather than in the weld throat, even though failure is most likely to occur in the throat. Thus, for joints involving approximately 6mm thick troughs and 6mm leg length fillet welds, the results suggest the use of Class G design stresses.

Increasing the weld size to 9mm, or using partial penetration welds, clearly resulted in some increase in strength. This was particularly apparent in the single axially loaded plate specimens (Fig. 7.13) but, to a lesser extent, was also found in the tests on repaired trough to cross-beam joints (Fig. 7.14). These results suggest that it would be appropriate to treat joints involving 6mm thick troughs and 9mm fillet welds or partial penetration welds, as Class F. However, any further improvement in classification with increasing weld size appears unlikely, since several of those specimens failed at the weld toe in the cross-beam.

### 7.3.2  Through troughs

With this type of detail the joint is effectively converted from the load carrying to the non-load carrying type, so that fatigue cracking in the weld is no longer a problem. The results shown in Fig. 7.24 suggest that, for joints that are welded all round, Class E is appropriate for the stress range in the trough apex with 6mm thick troughs; the weld size would not be expected to be relevant in this instance. However, if the weld is kept clear of the trough apex and restricted to the web the joint could be considered as being in Class D based on the stress in the region of the weld end. (In fact, the results were better than Class C but until confirmatory results are obtained that seems unduly optimistic).

Clearly both these classifications are distinctly superior to those for fitted troughs. However, the potential weak point of the through trough design is the upper end of the fillet weld on the trough web at the cope hole, if it exists. This should be treated as being in Class G (see Fig. 7.25). It would probably be better to omit the cope hole entirely and allow the welds to meet, but that type of detail has not been tested under the most severe type of loading likely to occur at that point; common sense suggests that it should probably be treated as being in Class F.

# 8 TROUGH TO DECK PLATE CONNECTION

One of the outcomes of the full-scale trial at Denham was that the strain measurements under actual traffic loading indicated that very high compressive stresses could occur in the deck plate transverse to the longitudinal trough stiffener near the weld. It was therefore thought that these compressive stresses, when combined with the, potentially, high tensile residual stresses due to welding, might cause fatigue failure in the deck plate from the toe of the weld. In addition, even though the highest transverse stresses were compressive and occurred when a wheel was positioned between troughs, the fact that the deck plate was continuous over several troughs meant that (smaller) tensile stresses could occur for other wheel positions (see Figs. 3.7 and 3.8). Taken together, therefore, the relevant stress ranges could be even higher.

In the light of the Denham strain measurements it was therefore decided that the fatigue strength of the trough to deck plate joint should be investigated more thoroughly. In the early stages of the test programme the significance of the bending stress in the web of the trough was not fully appreciated and most attention was paid to the bending stress in the deck plate. In this phase of the work tests were carried out both on simple idealised plate specimens (see Chapter 6) and also on small sections of deck. Subsequently, however, interest was concentrated primarily on the fatigue strength of the weld itself and in that case also the tests involved both simple specimens and sections of deck. Later still an extensive test programme was carried out to investigate possible methods of repairing the weld should that become necessary in service, as indeed it subsequently did in some instances.

## 8.1 Tests on trough to deck plate joints

The design of the test specimens used in this part of the work was based upon a typical orthotropic bridge deck with trapezoidal trough stiffeners as used for the Severn Crossing. Each specimen consisted of a 300mm length of a single trough with its associated deck plate, and Fig. 8.1(a) shows the dimensions which were common to all specimens. For reasons which will become apparent, the work involved three different modes of loading (see Fig. 8.1) as follows:

a)  on the deck plate at the trough centre-line, with the specimen supported symmetrically;
b)  as (a) but with the load applied to the trough;
c)  with the specimen supported unsymmetrically and the load applied unsymmetrically on the deck plate.

The initial part of the work, involving joints made with (nominally) 6mm leg length fillet welds, was primarily concerned with the derivation of the 'basic' fatigue strength of the joint. This included, in particular, tests at various stress ratios and an attempt to study the influence of

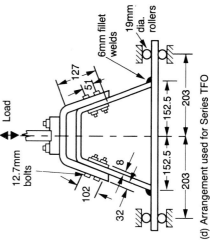

(c) Arrangement used for series TFA, TFB, TFC, and TFD

(d) Arrangement used for Series TFO

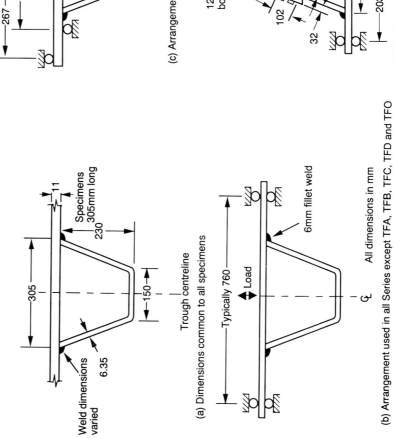

Trough centreline

(a) Dimensions common to all specimens

(b) Arrangement used in all Series except TFA, TFB, TFC, TFD and TFO

All dimensions in mm

98

Figure 8.1   Details of specimens and loading arrangements for trough to deck plate joint

residual stresses on the fatigue strength of this type of joint. The second part of the work was concerned with tests on several alternative repair weld geometries and procedures, which could be used if the need were ever to arise for the trough to deck weld to be repaired because of fatigue cracking occurring in service.

For convenience, a summary of all the test series used in the investigation of trough to deck plate joints is shown in Table 8.1. It will be seen that, to avoid confusion with the plate specimens, considered previously, each test series has been given an initial designation letter T (trough) followed either by F (fillet weld) or B (partial penetration weld). Finally, each individual series of general type TF or TB was identified by an additional letter and/or number (e.g. TFA1).

**TABLE 8.1    DETAILS OF TEST SERIES**

| Series | Description | Stress ratio | | Failure location |
|---|---|---|---|---|
| | | *Value* | *Position* | |
| TFE2 | 6mm downhand fillet weld. | 0 tension | weld root | Root |
| TFD4 | 9mm overhead fillet weld. | 0 tension | weld root | Root |
| TB1 | 6mm overhead fillet weld, 1/3 penetration, 4 passes | 0 tension | weld root | Root |
| TB2 | 9mm overhead fillet weld, 1/3 penetration, 6 passes | 0 tension | weld root | Root |
| TB3 | 6mm overhead fillet weld 1/3 penetration, 2 passes | 0 tension | weld root | Root |
| TB4 | Partial penetration, flux cored, 1 pass. | 0 tension | weld root | Root |
| TB5 | Partial penetration, flux cored, 2 passes. | 0 tension | weld root | Root |
| TB6 | Partial penetration, flux cored, 2 passes, but with deeper penetration. | O tension | weld root | Root |
| TB7 | 7mm throat overhead partial penetration weld, 3 passes | O tension | weld root | Weld toes |
| TFE1 | 6mm downhand fillet weld | O compression | weld root | Trough toe and root |
| TB3 | 6mm overhead fillet weld 1/3 penetration, 2 passes. | 0 tension | weld toe | trough toe |
| | | 0 tension | weld toe | Trough toe |
| TB3 | 6mm overhead fillet weld, 1/3 penetration, 2 passes, toe ground. | 0 tension | weld toe | Trough toe |
| TB3 | 6mm overhead fillet weld, 1/3 penetration, 2 passes but with ends peened. | 0 tension | weld toe | Trough toe |
| TB8 | 7mm throat overhead partial penetration, 3 passes. | 0 tension | weld toe | Trough toe |
| TB9 | 7mm throat overhead partial penetration weld, 3 passes, shot peened. | 0 tension | weld toe | All specimens |
| TB10 | 7mm throat overhead partial penetration weld, 3 passes, plasma dressed | O tension | weld toe | Deck toe |
| *Specimens loaded symetrically on trough (see fig 8.1)* | | | | |
| TF01 | | R=0 compression | deck toe | Root |
| | | R = 0 tension | root | Root |
| TF02 | | R = -1 | deck toe | Root |
| *Specimens loaded symmetrically on deck plate (see fig. 8.1)* | | | | |
| TFA1 | | -8.75 | deck | Root |
| TFA2 | | -1.41 | trough | Root |
| TFB | Spot heated at root. | -1.42 | trough | Root |
| TFC | Spot heated on weld surface | -1.42 | trough | Root |
| TFD | Root & surface spot heated | -1.42 | trough | Root |

99

It is important to recognise that all the work referred to in this chapter was concerned with specimens with no surfacing on the deck plate. The stress distributions which were used were also derived from measurements made on an unsurfaced deck panel. In view of this, the results probably represent a worst case situation and the stresses in a real bridge deck with surfacing may well be considerably lower.

## 8.2    Stress distribution

In the course of this part of the test programme three modes of failure were encountered, as follows:

a)      from the weld toe in the deck plate
b)      ·from the weld toe in the trough
c)      from the weld root through the weld throat.

Before considering the results, however, it is helpful to bring all of them to a common basis of stress. During the work, strains were monitored by means of electrical resistance strain gauges on each specimen, usually attached both to the web of the trough and to the deck plate. However, the gauge positions varied between different parts of the investigation so that, for the purposes of this summary, most of the results will be related to the stress 15mm from the weld root, or effectively a few millimetres away from the weld toe, in the trough.

The stress at that position can be deduced from stresses measured at other positions using the stress distributions which have been measured in various test series. Thus Fig. 8.2 shows the stress distributions measured in the trough in two series in which the load was applied unsymmetrically (TFA1 and TFA2) and in one series in which the load was applied on the deck plate at the centreline of the trough. The stress ranges at distances of 9, 15 and 32mm from the weld root, and the corresponding ratios between them, are given in Table 8.2 (the stress ranges at 15mm for the unsymmetrically loaded series having been determined by linear interpolation).

TABLE 8.2      STRESS DISTRIBUTION IN THE TROUGH WEB

| Position (see fig. 8.2) | Distance from weld root (mm) | Stress range, s (N/mm2) | | |
|---|---|---|---|---|
| | | Symmetrical load | Series TFA1 | Series TFA2 |
| C | 9 | 94 | 120 | 126 |
| X | 15 | 87 | 114 | 119 |
| D | 32 | 75 | 97 | 99 |
| E | 57 | | 81 | 84 |
| $\dfrac{\sigma_C}{\sigma_X}$ | | 1.08 | 1.05 | 1.06 |
| $\dfrac{\sigma_X}{\sigma_D}$ | | 1.16 | 1.17 | 1.19 |
| $\dfrac{\sigma_C}{\sigma_D}$ | | 1.25 | 1.23 | 1.26 |

100

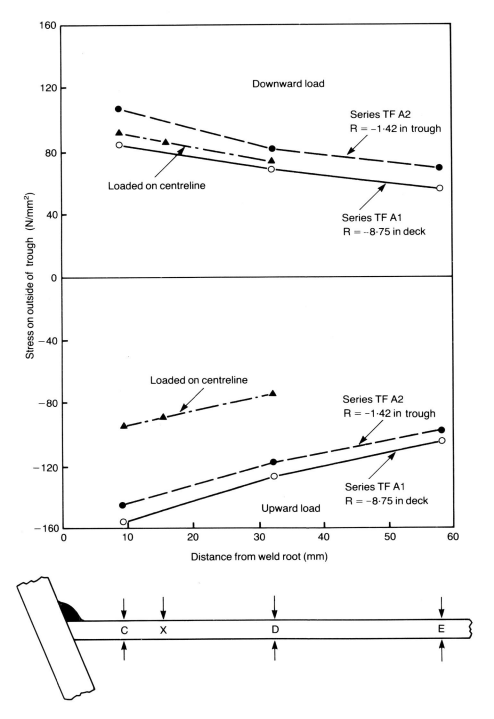

*Figure 8.2    Stress distribution on outside of trough web as determined from strain gauges*

On the basis of these results it seems reasonable to assume that, in the trough,

$$\frac{\sigma_c}{\sigma_x} = 1.06, \quad \frac{\sigma_x}{\sigma_D} = 1.19, \text{ and } \frac{\sigma_c}{\sigma_D} = 1.25 \text{ for all series} \qquad [8.1]$$

As far as the stress in the deck plate is concerned, comparative measurements of the stresses at the weld toes in the trough and in the deck plate were made in several test series, and the stress in the deck plate varied from 0.79 to 1.0 times the stress in the trough, with an average value of 0.83 for symmetrically loaded specimens. Much lower and higher values were obtained for the unsymmetrically loaded specimens in Series TFA1 and TFA2.

As will be seen later, it is also necessary, from the point of view of weld failure, to define the theoretical stress on the weld throat. This can be calculated in terms of the bending moment (M) and the direct force (P) in the web of the trough. Thus, working on the basis of the strain distributions in Series TFA1 and TFA2 (Fig. 8.2), and with the bending moment and direct force indicated in Fig. 8.3, we can assume:

a)  Plane of fracture = BD, the nominal throat size (t)

b)  The angles are as indicated in Fig. 8.3 (from simple geometry)

c)  The direct force, P, produces a bending moment at E, the centre of the fracture plane, of P x GE. For the loading shown this moment would give compression at the weld root and will be regarded as negative. A positive moment would result if P acted in the opposite direction.

d)  The direct force P also produces a direct stress on the plane of fracture of resolved value $P \cos \frac{\Theta}{2}$ over the area BD x weld leg length (l). For the force shown, the stress is compressive (negative).

e)  The bending moment, M, produces a bending moment of the same magnitude in the weld. Hence, the bending stress at the weld root, CY which for the bending moment shown is tensile (positive), is M/Z, where Z is section modulus of the fracture plane, that is

$$\frac{(DB)^3}{12} \times \frac{\text{weld length}}{DE} = \frac{t^3}{12} \times \frac{L}{0.5t} = \frac{t^2 L}{6} \qquad [8.2]$$

Now, from geometrical considerations,

$$FE = DE \sin\left(90 - \frac{\Theta}{2}\right) = \frac{t}{2} \cos \frac{\Theta}{2} \qquad [8.3]$$

and $\quad GE = GF + FE = \frac{T}{2} + \frac{t}{2} \cos \frac{\Theta}{2}$

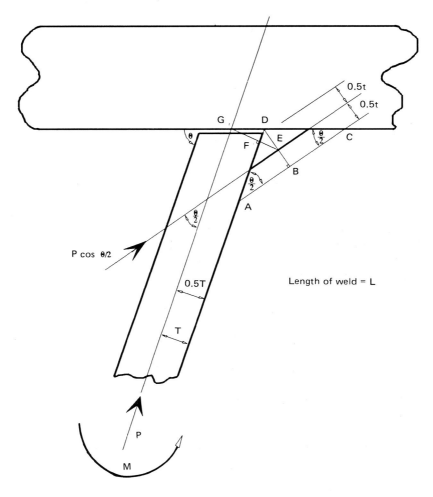

*Figure 8.3   Geometry of trough to deck plate joint assumed in calculation of stress in weld*

so that the resulting stress at the weld root is given by:

$$\sigma_{weld} \;=\; \underbrace{\frac{M}{Z} \;-\; \frac{P \times GE}{Z}}_{(bending)} \;-\; \underbrace{\frac{P\cos\dfrac{\Theta}{2}}{BD \times weld\ length}}_{(direct)}$$

$$=\; \frac{M - \dfrac{P}{2}\left(T + t\cos\dfrac{\Theta}{2}\right)}{\dfrac{t^{2}L}{6}} \;-\; \frac{P\cos\dfrac{\Theta}{2}}{tL} \qquad\qquad [8.4]$$

However, this equation can be rewritten in terms of stresses in the trough. Thus, M corresponds to a bending stress $\sigma_b$ which is given by M/Z, where Z corresponds to the trough section and is given by $LT^2/6$, so that

$$\sigma_b = \frac{6M}{LT^2}$$

or $\qquad M = \sigma_b \frac{LT^2}{6}$ [8.5]

and the direct force, P, corresponds to a direct stress, $\sigma_d$, given by

$$\sigma_d = \frac{P}{TL}$$

or $\qquad P = \sigma_d TL$ [8.6]

Hence, by substitution, equation [8.4] becomes

$$\sigma_{weld} = \frac{T^2}{t^2}\left[\sigma_b - \left(3 + 4\frac{t}{T}\cos\frac{\Theta}{2}\right)\sigma_d\right]$$ [8.7]

In this equation $\sigma_b$ and $\sigma_d$ are, of course, the nominal bending and direct stresses at the weld toe, but for all practical purposes it seems reasonable to assume them to be equivalent to the stresses 15mm from the weld root. Incidentally, if the bending moment 'closed' the weld and the direct force tended to 'open' it all the signs in equation [8.4] would be changed, so that equation [8.7] would give minus $\sigma_{weld}$.

In general, of course, it is easy to see that, on the grounds of equilibrium, there can be no direct stress in the web if the load is applied to the deckplate. The small direct stresses which were recorded in some of those specimens must, therefore, be attributed to experimental error. On the other hand, for the specimens which were loaded through the trough, there obviously was direct stress in the webs.

For the case of the unloaded trough we therefore have $\sigma_d = 0$ and

$$\sigma_{weld} = \frac{T^2}{t^2} \times \sigma_b$$ [8.8]

By similar reasoning it is easy to show that, for a partial penetration weld with depth of penetration (along the line of the junction between the trough and the deck plate) equal to p and with an external fillet of leg length l

104

$$\sigma_{weld} = \frac{T^2}{(1+p)^2 \sin^2 \dfrac{\Theta}{2}} \cdot \sigma_b \qquad\qquad [8.9]$$

With p = 0 this reduces to equation [8.8], since l Sin $\Theta$/2 = t in that instance.

In this particular work the trough thickness (T) was 6.35mm. Thus, for the specimens made with 1/4in. fillet welds (recorded in Table 8.1 as 6mm) the nominal weld throat thickness was t = 6.35 sin $\Theta$/2 = 3.74mm, which gives $T^2/t^2$=2.9. In practice the throat thicknesses for those specimens were greater than the calculated value, ranging typically from 4.2 to 5mm. As will be shown later, this difference has a significant effect on the fatigue test results and is a direct consequence of t being the dominant variable in equation [8.8].

## 8.3    Tests to derive the basic fatigue strength of the joint

As noted previously, this part of the work involved both tests at various stress ratios and also an attempt to study the influence of residual stresses on the fatigue strength and failure mode of this type of joint. At the start of the programme the main point of interest was the fatigue strength of the deck plate under the bending stress imposed by wheel loading. At this stage the importance of the bending stress in the trough was not appreciated.

Thus, as far as the deck was concerned, it was thought that conditions representative of service could be achieved by loading the specimen through the centre-line of the trough, and simply supporting the deck at points of contraflexure. These positions, found to be 50mm either side of the welds, were calculated on the assumption that the deck plate was continuous over several troughs, all of which were fixed, and that the load was applied mid-way between two troughs. The resulting testing arrangement, which involved the specimen being inverted, is shown in Fig. 8.1(d). Tests were then carried out on two series (TF01 and TF02), with the stress ratio at the weld toe in the deck plate being equal to -1 and to R = 0 (compression). The results, expressed in terms of the stress range at the weld toe in the deck plate, are shown in Fig. 8.4.

However, all the specimens of both series failed in the weld as a result of fatigue crack propagation from the weld root through the throat. Clearly this mode of failure occurred as a result of transverse bending in the trough; hence particular attention was then paid to the stresses occurring in the trough. Strain measurements were made on various specimens under different applied loads and it was found that there were indeed significant bending stresses in the trough, which could give tensile stresses at the weld root.

In view of the importance of the bending stresses in the trough, strains were measured on both the trough and deck plate of a sample bridge deck subjected to representative wheel loading. The results, plotted in the form of influence lines, are given in Fig. 8.5. (It should be noted that these influence lines were derived for slightly different gauge positions than those measured subsequently and shown in Fig. 3.7 and 3.8. Although the general form of the two sets of influence lines is similar there are differences in the absolute values of stress in the two cases.) They confirm that the bending stress in the trough can be significantly high compared with that in the deck plate.

105

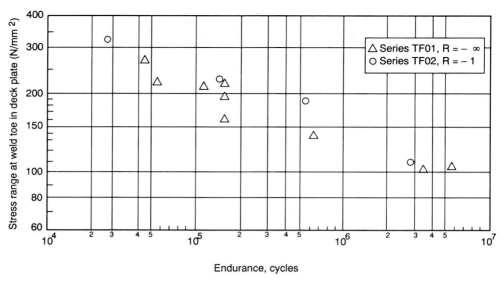

*Figure 8.4    Test results for specimens with 6mm fillet welds failing in the weld throat (phase I)*

Comparison of the results with those obtained from the specimens showed that the loading conditions used in the fatigue tests had not been too unrealistic. Nevertheless, it was decided to try to reproduce the stress distribution measured in the bridge deck in its most severe form. It was thought that this would be the condition in which the ratio stress range in trough/stress range in deck plate was a maximum, with the stress ratios in the two plates equivalent to the ratios of the minimum to maximum stress that could occur, that is -1.42 in the trough and -8.75 in the deck plate. In practice, the resulting loading would represent wheel loads alternately passing over the positions which gave the maximum and minimum stresses. (This could occur as a result of loading from adjacent vehicles, but not from adjacent axles on the same vehicle.)

Approximations of the required loading conditions were achieved using the test specimen and method of loading shown in Fig. 8.1(c), the load being applied on to the deck plate. These conditions were determined experimentally by applying static load off-centre and varying the support positions for tensile and compressive loading. It was not possible to obtain exact values of the stress ratios simultaneously, and so two sets of tests were carried out. In the first set (Series TFA1) the stress ratio in the deck plate was fixed at R = -8.75 and this gave values of between -1.73 and -8.3 in the trough. In the second set (Series TFA2) the stress ratio in the trough was fixed at R = -1.42 and this gave values of R between -1.67 and -6.4 in the deck plate. The tests were carried out under cyclic deflection loading and all connections between the loading point and specimen supports were through rollers. Since the specimens were loaded in an unsymmetrical way, only the weld closest to the loading point was stressed correctly. The strain in that region was monitored by gauges fixed with their centre-lines approximately 2.5mm from the weld toe in the deck plate and 32mm from the weld root in the trough.

The specimens all failed in the same way as those tested previously (i.e. through the weld throat from the root), thereby proving that the relevant stress is the bending stress in the weld. However, as noted previously, that is proportional to the stress range in the trough, so that the results are plotted in that form in Fig. 8.6 (using the interpolated stress range 15mm from the weld root).

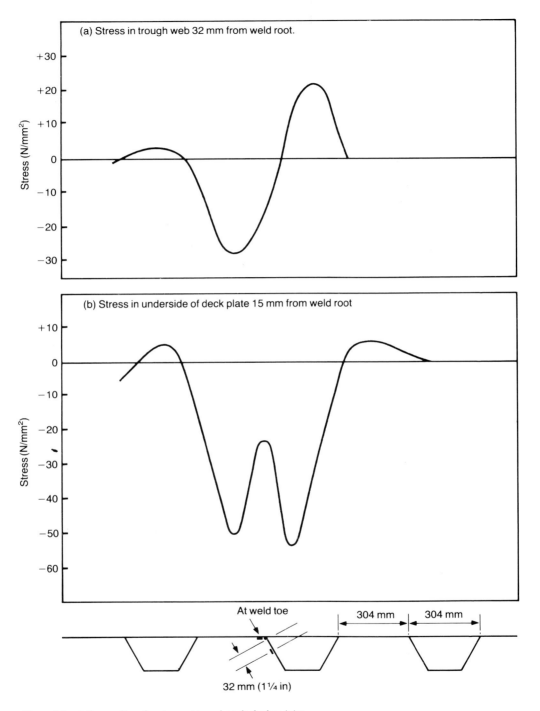

*Figure 8.5   Influence lines for stress at trough to deck plate joint*

107

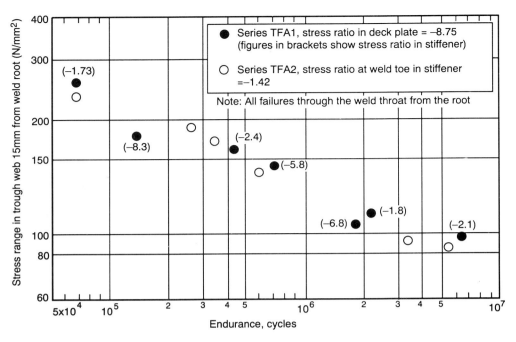

*Figure 8.6    Comparison of test results for trough to deck plate joints with 6mm fillet welds tested at different stress ratios (Phase 2)*

It will be seen that the results follow a well defined S-N curve with little scatter. It is interesting to note that the results do not appear to be influenced by the stress ratio, which varied between -1.4 and -8.3, in any consistent way. This range of R values may be increased by the addition of the earlier results shown in Fig. 8.4 and after conversion of those results to the same basis of stress, the combined set of results is shown in Fig. 8.7. It will be seen that, for values of R ranging from -1 to 0 (compression), there is little scatter, showing that, over that range of R values at least, the fatigue strength of the joint is independent of stress ratio and dependent only on stress range.

It seemed probable that this was due to the presence of high tensile residual stresses caused by welding. It is, of course, obvious that residual stresses of some sort must have existed, as in any welded joint; they are formed as a result of the large plastic deformations created by the thermal stresses during welding, but which remain after cooling. In general, provided that the structure or specimen is large enough to provide the necessary constraint to support them, the residual stresses parallel to a weld and adjacent to it will tend to be of yield stress magnitude in tension, and in some circumstances similar stresses may also exist transverse to the weld.

Residual stresses are, in some respects, comparable with a static mean stress, in that they can produce a substantial modification of the nominal applied stress cycle. Thus, in an as-welded structure with tensile residual stresses of yield stress magnitude, the actual stress cycle to which the material adjacent to the weld will be subjected will vary from yield stress tension downwards, regardless of the nominal stress ratio of the applied load. For example, if the nominal stress cycle is $+S_1$ to $-S_2$, giving a total range $(S_1 + S_2)$, the actual stress cycle will vary from $+S_y$ to $S_y - (S_1 + S_2)$. This is the reason why several current fatigue design rules express fatigue strength simply

108

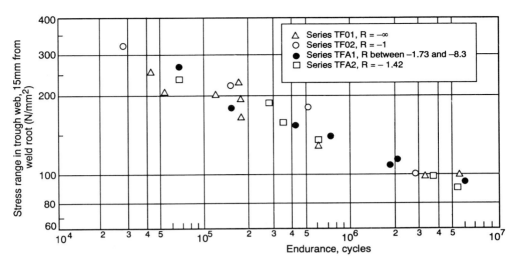

*Figure 8.7   Comparison of test results from figs. 8.4 and 8.6, plotted in terms of stress in the trough 15mm from the weld root (all failures through the weld throat)*

in terms of stress range with no reference to stress ratio. It also shows why it is possible for fatigue cracking to occur under compressive applied loading and, in the context of the tests on trough to deck joints described above, it shows why the variations in stress ratio may have had no effect.

However it was thought that the residual stress system around the joint might also have another important effect in that, if high tensile residual stresses happened to exist at either weld toe with compressive residual stresses at the root, failure might well occur at the toe rather than through the weld. Clearly that would be a more difficult problem from the point of view of subsequent repair.

Thus, in view of their potential importance, an attempt was made to study the influence of residual stresses on this type of joint. Although the magnitude and direction of the residual stresses in an actual bridge deck are not known and cannot be predicted with any accuracy, it at least seemed likely that they would be more severe than those in test specimens, on account of the size difference. Hence, various residual stress systems were induced in the test specimens by spot heating and they were fatigue tested under the same loading conditions as series TFA2, with the 'correct' stress ratio (R = -1.42) in the trough.

Since the main objective of this part of the work was to determine the effect on fatigue strength of the most severe residual stress system, maximum constraint was provided by spot heating on the centre line of the specimens. In fact three series were tested, which were spot heated, respectively:

a)   at the weld root (Series TFB),
b)   at the weld surface (Series TFC),
c)   at the weld root and on the surface simultaneously (Series TFD).

The results for all three series are shown in Fig. 8.8, where they are compared with the results

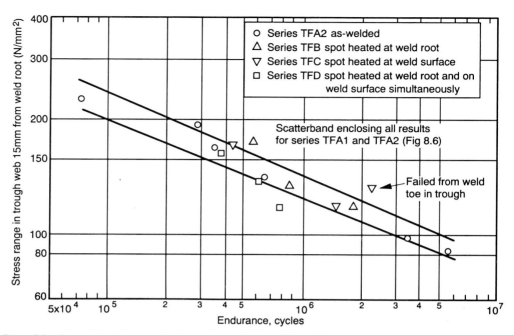

*Figure 8.8   Comparison of test results for specimens with 6mm fillet welds, but with various residual stress distributions, all tested at R=-1.42 in the trough*

for the as-welded specimens tested under the same stress ratio (Series TFA2). It will be seen that there was very little difference in strength between them.

It was, however, notable that in Series TFC, which was spot heated on the weld surface, all three specimens produced cracks at the weld toe, although in only one of them did that prove to be the primary mode of failure. In the other two series cracks seemed still to be restricted solely to the weld throat, initiating at the root. It seems clear, therefore, that these three series did confirm the potential importance of the residual stress system on the mode of failure.

Finally, some tests were carried out to supplement the earlier data with results which allowed for the influence of high residual welding stresses. In the earlier tests the loading had always been such as to cause the gap between the trough and the deck plate at the weld root both to open and close. In other words part of the stress cycle was always tensile at the root, tending to open the gap.

In an actual deck it was suspected that the presence of high tensile residual stresses at the weld root might result in a fully 'gap opening' cycle, even if the nominal stress ratio were partly compressive. One series (Series TFE2) was therefore tested with a fully tensile cycle at the root to simulate that condition. For comparison, a second series (Series TFE1) was tested with a fully 'gap closing' cycle. It was then anticipated that, if the two types of loading were found to give approximately the same fatigue test results, it would be reasonable to assume that a common S-N curve would apply for any stress ratio in a real bridge deck, where higher residual stresses should exist. In any case, the specimens tested under fully tensile stresses at the root should provide a reasonable lower limit strength for a similar joint containing high residual stresses and loaded in any way.

Hence, in terms of the bending stress in the sides of the trough near the weld toe, the stress ratios in the two series were either -∞ (zero to compression, corresponding to zero to tension at the weld root) or 0 (zero to tension, corresponding to compression at the weld root). The specimen type and loading arrangement are shown in Fig. 8.1(b), the load being applied to the deck plate through rollers. The loading conditions were selected to give equal stress ranges at the weld toes in the deck plate and trough. This is realistic in terms of the stresses actually experienced by the welded joint in practice (see Fig. 8.5). Also, in the event of residual stresses or the loading conditions used transferring the point of failure to a weld toe, there should be an equal chance of failure occurring in the deck plate and trough.

In fact four of the six specimens tested under compressive stress at the root failed from the weld toe in the trough, although in three of them cracks were also present at the weld root. For the specimens tested under 'gap opening' loading all failed in the weld, as before.

A summary of both sets of results is shown in Fig. 8.9, from which it will be seen that the specimens subjected to a cyclic compressive stress at the weld root fell on the upper limit of the scatter band for specimens loaded with only partial compressive stress at the root. On the other hand the results for specimens subjected to 'gap opening' loading fell slightly below the scatter band.

The difference between the results (for weld failure) obtained for fully compressive and fully tensile stress cycles at the weld root obviously reflects the influence of nominal stress ratio over the range of values relevant to a bridge deck. If the residual stresses in the specimens had been higher one would certainly expect the influence of applied stress ratio to diminish and all the results to be close to the lower limit in Fig. 8.9. This implies a fatigue strength at $2 \times 10^6$ cycles of about 81N/mm2 (based on the stress range 15mm from the weld root in the trough).

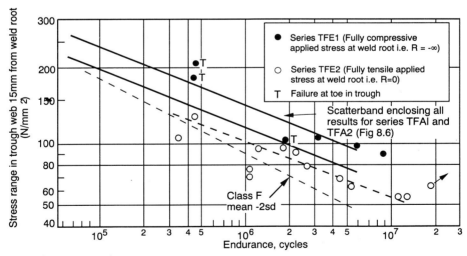

Figure 8.9    Test results for trough to deck plate specimens with 6mm fillet welds, with the weld root under fully tensile, or fully compressive loading

111

## 8.4   Tests on possible repair procedures

Given that the previous work had shown that cracking from the weld root through the throat was by far the most likely mode of failure, the work on possible repair procedures was concerned primarily with the repair of the weld and its subsequent fatigue strength.

The first option which was studied was the replacement of the 6mm fillet weld by a 9mm fillet. In order to simulate a repair as closely as possible, the specimens (Series TFF) were first welded with 6mm fillets. Those welds were then removed by grinding up to 1mm below the plate surface and were replaced by 9mm fillet welds made in 3 runs in the overhead position using basic electrodes which had been dried for one hour at 450°C.

For comparability with the previous tests on Series TFE2 the specimens were loaded as shown in Fig. 8.1(b), so that the stress cycle was fully tensile at the weld root. The results are shown in Fig: 8.10, from which it can be seen that the increase in weld size to 9mm resulted in a substantial increase in life, typically by an order of magnitude. However, the mode of failure was unchanged, with all specimens still failing from the weld root through the throat.

However, it was realised that this might not be the case in practice, since the loading on the bridge was likely to give an alternating stress at the weld toe rather than fully compressive loading as in the tests. That in turn would be expected to increase the chance of toe failure, particularly with such a large weld size in relation to the trough thickness of 6mm.

In any case, in spite of the good results obtained by increasing the size of the fillet weld, it was thought that the fatigue strength could also be increased, perhaps more efficiently, by increasing

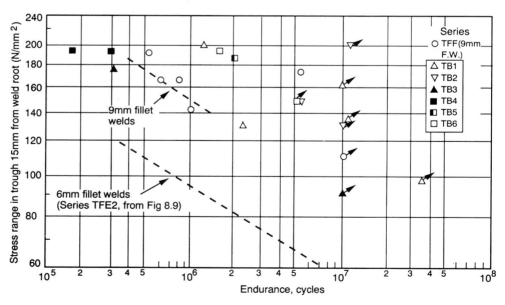

Figure 8.10   Test results for specimens with various weld sizes failing in the weld throat

112

the depth of weld root penetration. It was expected that the stress concentration at the root of a partial penetration weld would be less than that at the root of a fillet weld of the same size, so that better use would be made of the deposited weld metal in the case of the partial penetration weld. Therefore fatigue tests were carried out on joints made with partial penetration welds, in the hope that the fatigue strength of the joint could be extended beyond that obtained from the 9mm fillet welds, while at the same time making more efficient use of the deposited weld metal.

A variety of different weld preparations and procedures were tried, including both machine and hand ground preparations of various depths and welds made both by manual metal arc welding and by flux cored welding. A summary of the various preparations and weld dimensions of the joints tested is included in Table 8.1.

The first two series (Series TB1 and TB2) were made with machined edge preparations on the trough giving one-third penetration welds with leg lengths of 6 and 9mm respectively. At first sight the use of a machined preparation might seem surprising but it was envisaged that, if a significant amount of repair welding turned out to be necessary, it might be beneficial to make use of a purpose-built automated welding machine. If that option were adopted it was considered that it would also be possible to incorporate facilities for machining out the cracked weld prior to repair welding and that at the same time it should be possible to apply a preparation to the edge of the trough. Indeed it was estimated that, if necessary, it should be possible to obtain a weld root penetration of up to two-thirds of the trough thickness. For comparison, the third series (TB3) was made with a hand-ground edge preparation, using a 115mm diameter disc grinder, but it also had one-third penetration and a 6mm leg length fillet weld.

As was the case with the earlier 9mm fillet weld, the welds in each of these three series were made in the overhead position by manual metal arc (MMA) welding. The 6mm leg length welds made on machined edge preparations needed four weld passes, while the 9mm leg length welds needed six weld passes, as indicated in Table 8.1. However, with the need to try to reduce the welding time in mind, it was found possible to make the welds on the hand-ground preparation in only two weld passes.

The results obtained with these three series are included in Fig. 8.10, from which it can be seen that the specimens made with a machined preparation gave endurances which were rather greater than the original 'repaired' joints with a 9mm fillet weld, while the specimens made with a hand-ground preparation gave lives which were similar to those for the 9mm fillets.

Following these tests a further 3 series were tested in which the joints were made using flux cored welding, a process which offered considerable advantages over manual metal arc welding in that a high deposition rate and good penetration could be achieved. Three different procedures were used to produce joints, as noted in Table 8.1. First, Series TB4 specimens were produced using a single pass on to a deeper preparation than that used for Series TB3 joints. However, the resulting weld size was found to be insufficient from the point of view of fatigue failure in the weld throat and the Series TB5 specimen was fabricated using a similar procedure to Series TB4, but with two weld passes. Finally, Series TB6 specimens were fabricated using two weld passes on to a slightly deeper preparation than that used for Series TB4 and TB5 joints.

The results for these three series are also shown in Fig. 8.10, and the relatively poor strength associated with series TB4 (the single pass weld) is very obvious. However, the results obtained from Series TB5 and TB6 showed that satisfactory fatigue strength could be obtained by making the weld in two passes with a weld throat size of the order of 7-8mm. At that time, however, it became apparent that, with the particular joint geometry that was involved, the flux cored welding process tended to deposit welds with inadequate fracture toughness, so that particular approach to the problem was abandoned.

However, in the light of the information that a weld with a throat thickness of 7mm appeared to be satisfactory, a further set of specimens (Series TB7) was fabricated with partial penetration MMA overhead welds with a 7mm throat size. In making these specimens the objective was to derive a procedure with the minimum number of weld passes, in order to reduce cost and welding time, and also using a single size of electrode, so as to avoid possible confusion on site. In fact, satisfactory results were obtained using a 3 pass procedure with 3.25mm diameter low hydrogen electrodes on to a 90° edge preparation. Care was needed in positioning the weld beads to ensure that the required throat thickness was achieved; incorrect positioning could produce an uneven weld usually with a larger leg on the deck plate than on the trough, with inadequate throat thickness. A similar result was obtained if the second weld pass was made on the trough side of the weld rather than the deck.

In this Series the only specimen which failed had fatigue cracks at both weld toes, the primary failure being in the trough. The results are shown in Fig. 8.13. This was the first time that a specimen tested with tensile stress at the root did not fail through the weld throat.

It was then decided to check the behaviour of both the Series TB3 joints (MMA welds made on a hand-ground preparation) and of the Series TB7 joints when they were subjected to a zero-tension stress cycle at the toe and compressive loading at the root (Series TB8). This was achieved by reversing the direction of loading and applying it as in Series TFE1. As was expected, both series gave failures through the trough from the weld toe and the results are summarised in Fig. 8.11, but the lives achieved were rather less than were thought, at that time, to be required.

In view of this situation consideration was given to the possible use of various fatigue strength improvement techniques, such as toe grinding, plasma dressing and shot peening, and to this end specimens of the same type as Series 3 were treated and tested under zero-tension loading at the weld toe.

As far as toe grinding was concerned the procedure used was to grind, with a hand-held disc grinder, to such a depth that the original weld toe and any undercut were completely removed. In practice this usually meant that approximately 0.5mm of trough plate thickness was removed. In order to simulate site conditions, the toe grinding operation was carried out in the overhead position. A typical ground weld toe is shown in Fig. 8.16. It may be noted that the grinding operation reduced the effective weld throat size significantly, typically from 6mm to 3.5mm. This means that the fatigue strength of the joint from the viewpoint of weld throat failure is likely to have been reduced as a result of toe grinding.

In the initial fatigue tests carried out on three toe-ground joints (Series TB3G1), fatigue cracking initiated near the ends of the welds. Examination of those regions revealed that the weld size was somewhat smaller than required and that the toe grinding had reduced it further. Therefore, three more specimens (Series TB3G2) were prepared and, in order to prevent preferential initiation at the weld ends, the weld toe adjacent to the ends was also hammer peened.

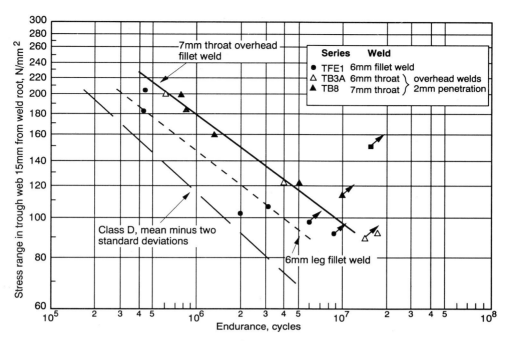

*Figure 8.11  Test results for specimens failing from the weld toe in the trough (R=0, ie tension, at toe)*

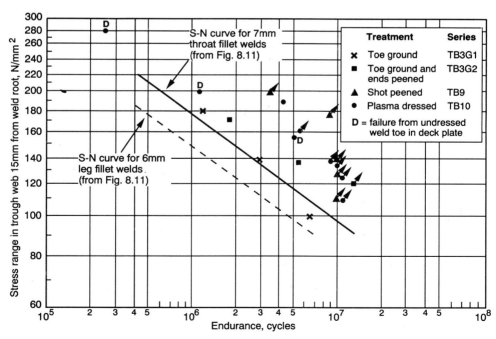

*Figure 8.12  Test results for specimens with treated welds intended to fail from the weld toe in the trough (R=0 at toe)*

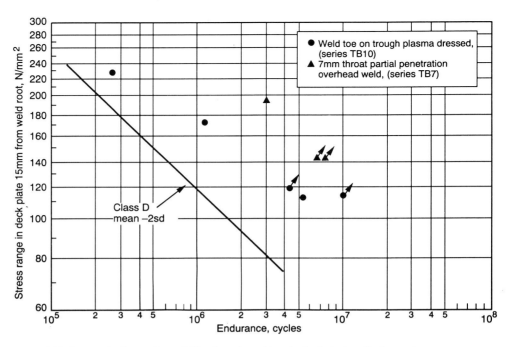

*Figure 8.13   Test results for specimens failing from the weld toe in the deck plate (R=0 at toe)*

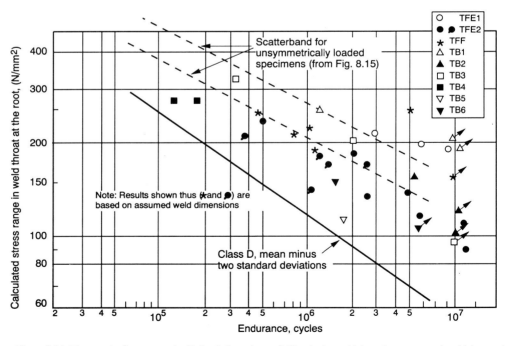

*Figure 8.14   Test results for symmetrically loaded specimens failing in the weld, based on measured weld throat size*

116

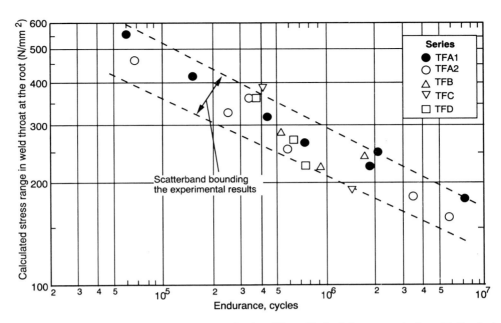

*Figure 8.15 Test results for specimens with (nominally) 6mm fillet welds, loaded unsymmetrically and failing in the weld, based on measured weld throat size.*

In view of this and the fact that, in any case (see Fig. 8.12), toe grinding did not produce a large improvement in fatigue strength from the point of view of toe failure, it was concluded that weld toe grinding using a disc grinder was unlikely to be suitable for application on a bridge.

With regard to the plasma dressed specimens (Series TB10), the plasma dressing was carried out with the specimen in the same position as for the repair welding, so that an overhead operation was required. Although the operation can be carried out automatically, this may not prove to be feasible on a bridge and therefore it was carried out manually. The plasma dressing conditions were as follows:

| | |
|---|---|
| Position | Overhead (deck plate horizontal) |
| Constricting nozzle | 3.2mm diameter |
| Plasma gas | Argon at 30 psi and 0.95l/min. |
| Shielding gas | Argon/5% hydrogen at 300psi and 9.5l/min. |
| Nozzle/weld toe dist. | 10mm approximately |
| Torch/workpiece geometry | Leading by approximately 25°. |
| Welding current | 115A |
| Arc voltage | 18-25V |
| Travel speed | 85-100mm/min. |

Prior to dressing, the weld was cleaned by wire brushing, an operation which proved to be necessary to avoid porosity and the occurrence of slag in the dressed region. Initially, only the weld toe on the trough was dressed but, subsequently, the weld toes on the deck plates of three specimens were also dressed. From the practical viewpoint, it may be noted that a number of problems were experienced by the operator. Care was needed to maintain sufficient distance

117

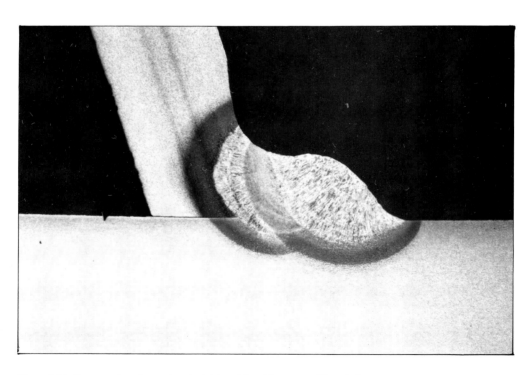

*Figure 8.16  Cross section of trough to deck joint with weld toe treated by grinding*

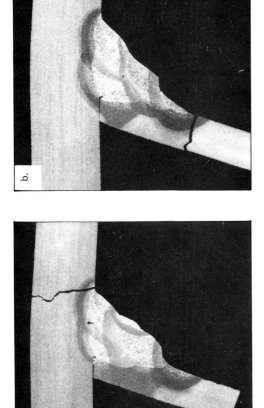

a. Failure from as-repaired weld toe in deck, x1.9

b. Failure from plasma dressed toe in stiffener, x1.9

c. Both toes plasma dressed, specimen unbroken after $10^7$ cycles, x1.9

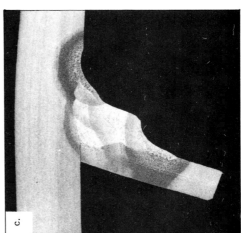

*Figure 8.17  Cross sections of trough to deck joints with plasma dressed welds*

119

between the plasma torch and the workpiece to avoid nozzle burn-out due to reflected heat. Secondly, it proved necessary to interrupt the operation at approximately 150mm intervals for the operator to change his stance; this introduces the possibility of stop/start defects. Finally, the operation was found to be particularly tiring due to the awkward position and heat produced. It seems likely, however, that these difficulties could be reduced or eliminated by introducing a wheel tracking support system for the plasma torch, or even a purpose-built mechanised system.

Nevertheless, in spite of the difficulties encountered, the results (Fig. 8.12) were encouraging and only one plasma dressed specimen failed from the expected location, that is the weld toe in the trough. However, three specimens failed from the weld toe in the deck plate, a region which had not been plasma dressed. Unfortunately, due to the fact that several specimens were under test at the same time, by the time it was realised that this mode of failure was likely to occur, seven tests were complete or nearing completion. At this stage, the remaining three specimens were plasma dressed on the deck plate weld toe and none of them failed. Examples of sections through the two types of plasma dressed specimens are shown in Fig. 8.17.

As far as the shot peened joints (Series TB9) are concerned, the peening conditions complied with the US Defence Department Military Specification 'Shot peening of metal parts' MIL-S-13165B, 1979. A steel shot described as MI 230H was used. This has a diameter of approximately 0.023in. (0.6mm) and a hardness of 55-65 Rockwell C. The intensity of peening, given as the arc height of a Type 2 Almen strip, was 0.012-0.016in. (0.30-0.41mm) and this was achieved in two passes with a shot velocity of approximately 200m/sec. The peening operation was carried out in a workshop under controlled conditions. It seems likely that similar treatment could be introduced on-site using a semi-automatic system but, clearly, this would need to be checked if shot peening were finally chosen as the technique to be used on a bridge. The shot peening covered the whole weld and extended approximately 30mm either side of it.

As can be seen from Fig. 8.12, none of the shot peened specimens failed and the improvement in life which was obtained appeared to be similar to that obtained by plasma dressing. From the practical viewpoint, however, the treatment is noisy and may be unwelcome on environmental grounds.

In summary, therefore, it appeared that the most satisfactory improvement technique was likely to be plasma dressing but that, if treatment were applied solely to the weld toe on the trough, failure was liable to be transferred to the weld toe on the deck plate.

In the light of all the results for trough to deck plate welds outlined in this Chapter, it is interesting to reconsider the results for each mode of failure in turn with a view to defining the relevant implications with regard to design stresses.

## 8.5    Failure from the weld toe in the trough

The results for specimens giving this mode of failure are summarised in Fig. 8.11. It will be noted that trough toe failure was only obtained in test series which were loaded symmetrically and downwards on the deck plate so as to give tensile stresses at the toe and compressive stresses at the weld root.

From Fig. 8.11 there seems to be a clear indication of increasing fatigue strength with an increase in weld size. Owing to the relatively small number of specimens which were tested it is difficult to define accurate 'strengths', particularly for the joints with 6mm fillet welds, but at $2 \times 10^6$ cycles they were approximately:

| | |
|---|---|
| 6mm leg length fillet weld | 120N/mm2 |
| 7mm throat fillet with 2mm penetration | 145N/mm2 |

Although the use of thicker troughs might be expected to give lower strengths it appears realistic, for the time being, to base the design of this joint (for this mode of failure) on the Class D design curve, the relevant stress being that in the trough web 15mm from the weld root (see Fig. 8.11).

## 8.6   Failure from the weld toe in the deck plate

Extremely few specimens suffered this mode of failure, but the results for those which did are summarised in Fig. 8.13. The small number of results is, however, not surprising. In the first place, the majority of the tests were carried out with compressive stresses at the weld toe (opening at the weld root) and they nearly all failed through the weld, while for the specimens which were tested with tension at the toe, the stress in the deck plate was lower than the stress in the trough so that most of those specimens failed in the trough.

However, as discussed previously, the specimens which were plasma dressed only at the weld toe in the trough did tend to fail at the weld toe in the deck plate, the strength at $2 \times 10^6$ cycles again being about 140N/mm2. Hence, once again, design on the basis of the stress range in the trough 15mm from the weld root complying with the Class D design curve would appear to be realistic. The single failure for a completely untreated weld shown in Fig. 8.13 refers to a specimen tested with compressive stresses at the weld toe.

## 8.7   Failure through the weld throat from the root

The initial attempt to correlate the results for this mode of failure was based upon the nominal weld size and the corresponding nominal stress at the weld root derived from equation [8.8]. However the results, particularly for the symmetrically loaded specimens, showed a very large degree of scatter and were therefore unhelpful for design purposes. Similarly, expressing the results in terms of the stress in the trough 15mm from the weld root (see Fig. 8.10) was also unhelpful, primarily because the fatigue strength relating to weld throat failure was clearly a function of the size of the weld throat. From Fig. 8.9 it would seem reasonable to base the design of joints made with 6mm fillet welds on Class F for the stress in the trough 15mm from the weld root; for larger welds, however, the strength is higher.

In view of the lack of success with those correlations, the results were replotted in terms of the calculated stress at the weld root based upon the measured, rather than the nominal, weld throat dimensions (see Figs 8.14 and 8.15). It will be seen in Fig. 8.14 that, apart from the results for

Series TFE1 (zero to compression at the root), there was reasonable agreement between all the results in terms of the stress on the weld throat. Similarly, there was reasonable agreement between the results for symmetrically and unsymmetrically loaded joints. Thus the results in Fig. 8.14 provide the basis for a design S-N curve for trough to deck plate welds for weld throat failure. Comparing them with existing design curves (see Fig. 8.14) suggests that the Class D curve would be suitable. On the other hand it would be wise to bear in mind that the experimental data relate to a limited range of geometries so that, at this stage, that design curve should only be assumed to be applicable to weld throat thicknesses up to 9mm, the maximum tested.

A direct comparison can, however, be made between the results for Series TFE1 and TFE2 and the unsymmetrically loaded joints, since they all had the same joint geometry. The difference between them was that in Series TFE1 the weld root was subjected to zero to compression stresses while in Series TFE2 the loading was R = 0 tensile; the unsymmetrically loaded specimens were of course tested at an intermediate stress ratio (namely R = -1.42). It is clear from Fig. 8.14 that Series TFE2 gave a lower strength than the unsymmetrically loaded specimens while Series TFE1 gave a higher strength. Nevertheless, it is worth noting that some failures still occurred in the weld even under zero to compression loading (just as some specimens produced cracks at the weld toe when that was subjected to zero to compression loading). Very approximately, the fatigue strengths (stress ranges) at 2 x $10^6$ cycles for the various stress ratios are given in Table 8.3.

**TABLE 8.3    FATIGUE STRENGTH AT DIFFERENT STRESS RATIOS**

| Stress ratio (R) | Series | Fatigue strength at 2x10⁶ cycles (N/mm2) |
|---|---|---|
| R = 0 (tension) | TFE2 | 160 |
| R = -1.42 | See fig 8.17 | 210 |
| R = 0 (compression) | TFE1 | 250 |

From these results it is clear that, in the particular specimens which were tested, the stress ratio at the weld root had a very significant influence on fatigue strength. However, in actual structures, it would have to be expected that higher tensile residual stresses would exist at the root. This would ensure the fatigue lives obtained under zero to compression loading would almost certainly be similar to those obtained under tensile loading. It is therefore recommended that the Class D design curve should be applied to all stress ratios (i.e. that fatigue strength should, as in other types of joint in the as-welded condition, be assumed to be independent of stress ratio).

With regard to the influence of weld geometry, which was the main point of concern in the tests on Series 1-6, it has to be concluded that too few specimens were tested to enable valid conclusions to be reached. Nevertheless, based upon the bending stress in the trough (as opposed to the stress in the weld), it is quite obvious from Fig. 8.10 that fatigue strength is increased by increasing the weld throat, whether that be done by introducing some degree of weld penetration or merely by increasing the weld size. Indeed, it seems obvious that that should be a design requirement. Based on the stress at the weld root (Fig. 8.14), one can only conclude, at this stage, that the lower limit of the scatter band at 2 x $10^6$ cycles is at about 115N/mm2. Clearly this is far above the Class W design stress (43N/mm2), although for design purposes care should obviously be taken to calculate the relevant weld throat stress in the same way as used for the analysis of the experimental data. In terms of the design S-N curves in BS 5400 the use of Class C would lead to a few of the test results in Fig. 8.14 falling below the mean -2 standard deviations design curve. Hence, once again, Class D seems to be appropriate.

# 9  DECK TO PLATE CONNECTIONS

Apart from the joints between the longitudinal trough stiffeners and the deck, orthotropic decks often have two other types of plate to deck joints, one between the deck and the cross-beams and the other between longitudinal box webs and the deck. Although these two joints have many features in common the stress conditions are different. It is therefore convenient to consider them separately.

## 9.1    Deck to cross-beam joint

Transverse cross-beams are generally connected to the deck by means of double fillet welds and in general it is not difficult to provide welds that are sufficiently large to avoid failure in the weld throat. However that leaves open the possibility of failure from the weld toe, either in the cross-beam or the deck.

As described in Chapter 3, influence lines for this joint show that, as a wheel passes, there is a single alternating cycle at the weld toe on the cross-beam while the toe on the deck plate is subjected to a major fully compressive cycle and an associated minor cycle. The maximum difference between these two cycles occurs when the wheel is directly over the cross-beam.

In order to simulate this type of loading in the laboratory the test specimens (Fig.9.1(a)) were loaded by 2 actuators, 150° out of phase, so that the first actuator was still applying some load when the second started to apply its load. A typical output from the strain gauges on the deck and cross-beam is shown in Fig.9.1(b).

The specimens were made with two different weld sizes, 6 and 9-10mm, and the majority failed from the weld toe in the cross-beam. As can be seen from Fig.9.2, in terms of the stress range in the cross-beam there was little difference in strength between the two weld sizes, both giving strengths well above Class D in BS 5400.

Figure 9.2 also shows some results for specimens which were needle peened in four passes at each weld toe. Clearly this treatment produced a large improvement in life, typically by a factor of seven as compared with that for the joints with the larger welds. Furthermore no fatigue cracking was found in specimens tested at stress ranges up to 260N/mm2.

The results for the untreated joints are repeated, in terms of the peak stress range (ignoring the small cycle) in the deck plate, in Fig.9.3. Once again it can be seen that Class D seems to be an appropriate classification, and that is confirmed by the results of the tests on simple specimens of types PD1 and PD2 (see Fig.6.4); for convenience the relevant results are re-produced in Fig. 9.4.

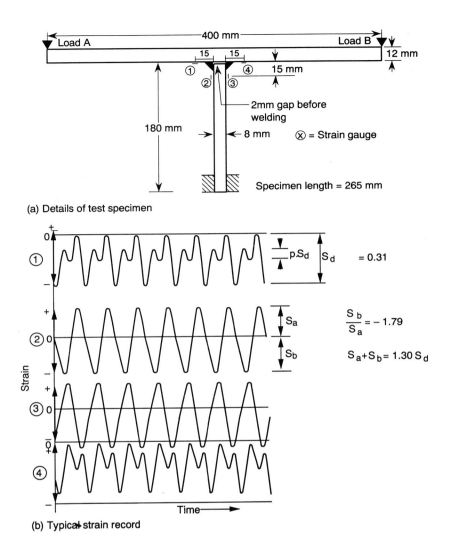

(a) Details of test specimen

(b) Typical strain record

*Figure 9.1    Tests on specimens representing the cross-beam to deck joint*

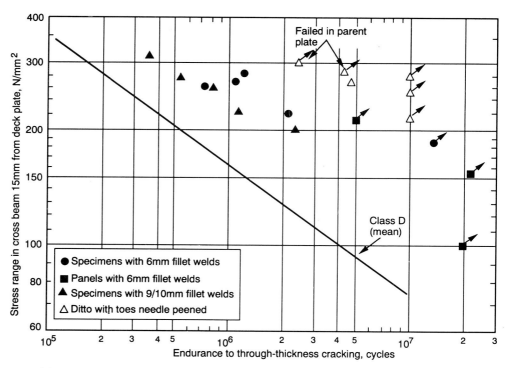

*Figure 9.2    Test results for cross-beam to deck joint for failure at the weld toe in the cross-beam*

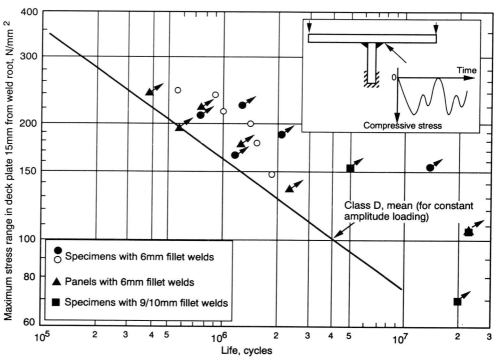

*Figure 9.3    Test results for cross-beam to deck joint for failure at the weld toe in the deck plate*

126

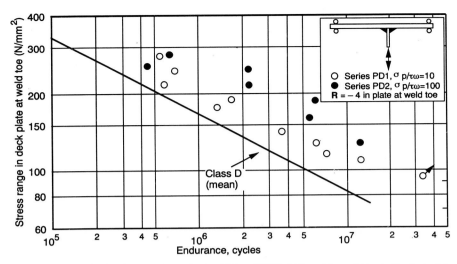

*Figure 9.4    Test results for plate specimens (series PD1 and PD2) failing at the weld toe in the deck plate*

## 9.2   Longitudinal web to deck welds

In some types of bridge design, particularly those consisting of a box girder with an orthotropic deck as the top flange, it is common for the longitudinal webs of the box to be welded to the deck plate midway between two adjacent longitudinal troughs (see Fig.9.5). The joint is usually made with two fillet welds and so is geometrically similar to the cross-beam to deck joint, but the influence lines due to wheel loading are different (Fig.9.6).

The main differences are:-

(a)     that the minor stress cycle in the deck plate is not present in the web to deck joint. In this respect the weld toe on the deck is less severely stressed than is the deck to cross-beam joint.

(b)     that the stress in the web is entirely tensile or compressive (depending on the transverse position of the wheel) rather than alternating, as in the cross-beam. In fact, however, when residual stresses are taken into account it is probable that the resulting stress cycles are similar in the two joints.

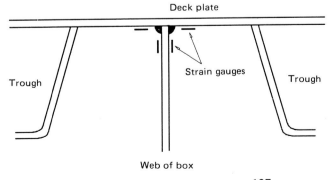

*Figure 9.5
General arrangement of
longitudinal web to deck joint,
showing position of strain gauges*

127

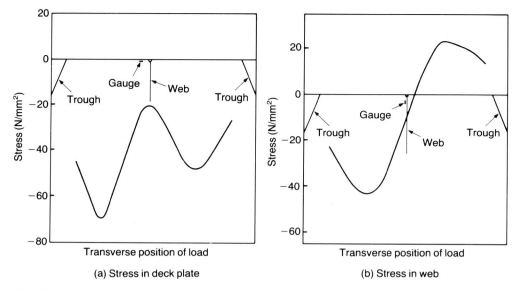

*Figure 9.6    Transverse influence lines for stress at web to deck joint for a 30kN single wheel load*

Although the web to deck joint has not specifically been tested it is clear that, under the influence of wheel loading, this type of joint is subjected primarily to bending of the deck plate over the stiffener, and fatigue tests relevant to this mode of loading have already been discussed in Chapter 6 (see specimens of Types PA, PD and PF, and in relation to the cross-beam to deck joint. The two types of joint appear to be so similar that it seem reasonable that they should be in the same class (i.e. Class D).

The main problem with this particular joint is that it tends to create a 'hard spot' in the deck, a common result of which is for the surfacing to crack immediately above the joint after only a short period in service. The subsequent reduction of composite action from the surfacing then increases the stresses in the joint, although they are still considerably less than in an unsurfaced deck; in addition, the top side of the deck plate becomes exposed to corrosion from water penetration through the cracked surfacing.

Some measure of the effect of uncracked and cracked surfacings on the fatigue life of this joint was obtained by strain gauge measurements under the various conditions, followed by calculations of the life using the influence lines so derived. Unfortunately it was not possible to obtain direct comparability between the various conditions, partly because some of the calculations were based upon theoretical, and some on actual, traffic spectra and partly because, in some of the tests, part of the influence line could not be derived experimentally and therefore had to be obtained by extrapolation. However after making reasonable corrections for these difficulties the calculated proportionate lives were:-

| | |
|---|---|
| Unsurfaced deck | 1.0 |
| Deck surfaced and uncracked | 7.6 |
| Deck surfaced but cracked | 2.15 |

128

These results demonstrate, very dramatically, that a suitable surfacing system can lead to large increases in life of many welded joints close to the deck plate; indeed this probably explains why many joints in existing decks are apparently free of fatigue cracks. On the other hand they also show that subsequent cracking of the surfacing can lead to a very severe decrease in strength and effective loss of most of the beneficial effect of surfacing.

In view of this situation two possible methods of strengthening the longitudinal web to deck joint were considered. The first was to attach two rows of 600 x 270mm plates to the underside of the deck, adjacent to the web, using epoxy adhesive. However it was found difficult to fit the plates in the correct position due to the uneven surface and also because of slippage when attempts were made to apply pressure to support the plates; indeed it was found that the thickness of the adhesive ranged from less than 1mm to more than 6mm. In view of these difficulties that particular possible method of improvement was abandoned.

The second method was to weld 6mm thick stiffening plates between the box web and the deck, as shown in Fig.9.7. In fact the region between two adjacent cross-beams was treated by installing three plates on each side of the web, with a gap of 50mm between them. The gaps were subsequently covered by 250 x 200 x 6mm overlapping plates fillet welded into place. This produced a large reduction in stress in the deck adjacent to the web, to such an extent that cracking of the surfacing at that point seems unlikely to occur. Nevertheless it is still possible that cracking of the surfacing might merely be transferred to a new location over the line of the stiffening plate to deck connection, although that is unlikely, as the stresses in that location are relatively low. However, in the absence of such cracking, the new reduced stresses suggest that the life of the joint with this type of strengthening should be about four times that of the unstrengthened joint with uncracked surfacing (i.e. about 30 times the life of an unsurfaced deck). Clearly this is an improvement method that is worthy of serious consideration, and it is in fact being used on at least one UK bridge.

There is, however, a simpler and cheaper method that can be used in many instances. Since the transverse location of the wheel tracks has a significant effect on the life of this joint the life can be improved by moving the transverse location of the traffic lanes, and hence of the wheel tracks. They need to be positioned as far as possible from the joint. Nevertheless a problem with this solution is that the wheel lanes might shift with time (say 50 years hence).

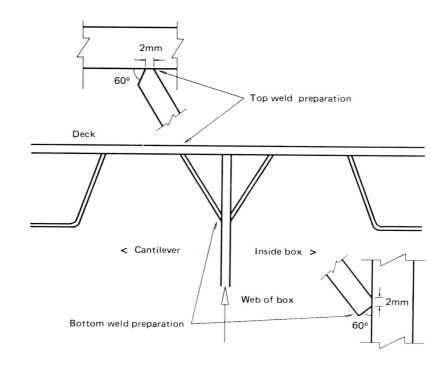

2mm

60°

Top weld preparation

Deck

< Cantilever

Inside box >

Web of box

Bottom weld preparation

2mm

60°

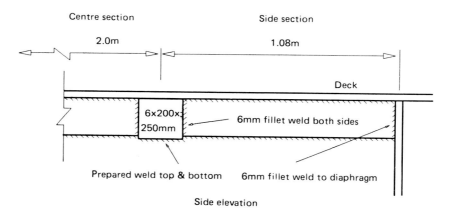

Centre section

Side section

2.0m

1.08m

Deck

6x200x
250mm

6mm fillet weld both sides

Prepared weld top & bottom

6mm fillet weld to diaphragm

Side elevation

*Figure 9.7   Method of strengthening longitudinal web to deck joint by means of welded stiffeners*

130

# 10 SPLICE JOINTS IN LONGITUDINAL STIFFENERS

In many of the earlier designs of orthotropic decks the longitudinal trough stiffeners were fitted between the cross-beams and attached to them by fillet welds. However, as shown previously, this type of joint is prone to fatigue cracking through the weld throat. Later, therefore, that type of design has tended to be abandoned in favour of a design in which cut-outs are left in the cross-beam to fit around the troughs which are made continuous. This involves making splice joints in the troughs, away from the cross-beams, usually by positional site welding. Indeed, this type of joint can account for 40% of site welding and in very long spans up to 5000 such joints may be required. Their adequacy is therefore of some importance.

There are three types of welded splice joint which have been used to make site connections between adjacent lengths of trough. The essential features of each are shown in Fig. 10.1 and they are:

i)      A single lap joint in which a V shaped cover plate is fitted over the troughs and fillet welded in place.
ii)     A double lap joint in which cover plates are fitted inside and outside the troughs and fillet welded in place.
iii)    A butt welded splice in which a backing strip is provided and an infill piece is fitted between the troughs and butt welded in place.

A limited number of tests was carried out on each of these three variants and in the case of the butt welded splice the programme involved three different welding procedures. For each type of joint the specimens consisted of a single trough, with a splice, and an associated section of deck plate which was 560-600mm wide. The test set-up was typically as shown in Fig. 10.2, although in some instances 3 point, rather than 4 point, bending was used.

Since several of the tests were carried out with the objective of simulating conditions in particular bridges, in which the splices were positioned at different distances from the adjacent cross-beam, they were at several different stress ratios. Nevertheless, since it has usually been found that the fatigue strength of as-welded joints is insensitive to stress ratio, due to the presence of high tensile residual stresses, it seems reasonable to compare all the results on the basis of stress range. They are therefore summarised in Fig. 10.3 in terms of the measured stress range 25mm from the toe of the splice weld at the apex of the trough, that being the stress which would be used in design.

The most obvious feature of the results is the relatively low strength of the splice made with a single lap fillet weld. In these joints the basic trough was 6mm thick, the splice plate was 8mm thick and the leg length of the fillet welds was also 8mm. Given that all the failures were through the weld throat from the root, it is clear that some improvement in strength might be expected by increasing the weld size, and the corresponding thickness of the splice plate, but the degree of improvement required in order for such a joint to reach that of the other joints is clearly

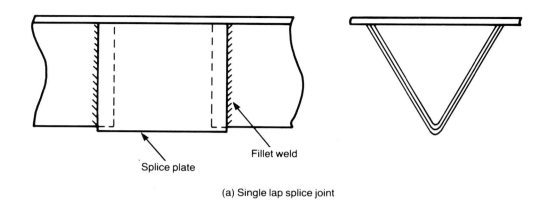

(a) Single lap splice joint

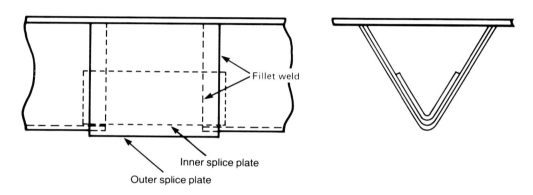

(b) Double lap splice joint

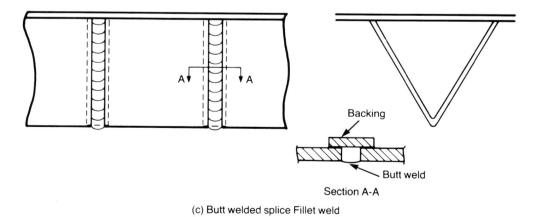

(c) Butt welded splice Fillet weld

*Figure 10.1  Types of welded trough splice joint*

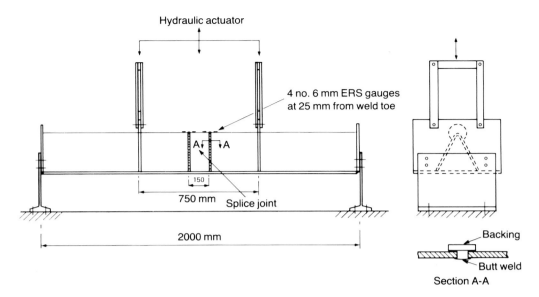

*Figure 10.2  Test specimen and loading arrangement for splice joint*

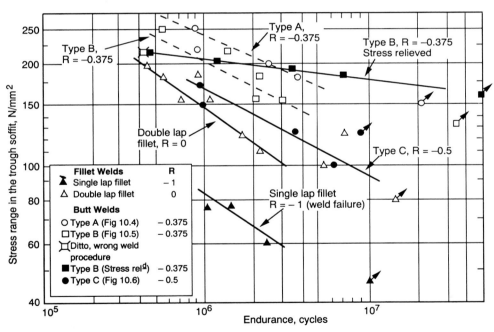

*Figure 10.3  Test results for welded splice joints in 4 point bending.*

unattainable. The strength of the splice made with double lap fillet welds is at least twice that of the single lap joint; indeed, rather surprisingly, it approaches that for the various butt welded splices, particularly when it is remembered that it was the only joint tested under fully tensile loading (R = 0).

133

As far as the butt welded splices are concerned, it is clear that all the results fall into a fairly broad scatter band but that there are significant differences in strength between the various test series. Thus, at 2 x 10⁶ cycles, the strengths of the 3 series which were not stress relieved were approximately:

Type A 205 N/mm2.
Type B 170 N/mm2.
Type C 140 N/mm2.

The differences between these three types lay in the welding procedure and in the backing provided for the butt welds.

In the splice joint modelled by the series A specimens the ends of the longitudinal trough stiffeners were sealed to prevent corrosion by 19mm thick plates which fitted inside the ends of the troughs and projected so that the edge of the plate formed a backing for the splice joint butt weld. The welds were made in 3 passes with the weld runs starting alternately to either side of the apex of the trough. This was done to avoid concentrating the defects associated with weld start/stop positions at the most highly stressed point, the apex. Details of the series A joint are given in Fig. 10.4.

In Series B a simpler welding procedure was used (see Fig. 10.5) in which all the weld runs started at the apex of the trough. This was expected to lead to higher productivity and lower defect rates since it was found that the staggered weld start procedure used in Series A was difficult and could lead to defects as the welder tried to manipulate the electrode around the apex.

For Series C (Fig. 10.6) a three pass butt weld in a rectangular preparation was specified, but in this case diaphragm plates were not used to seal the ends of the troughs so a 30 x 6mm backing strip was provided for the butt welds. The backing strip was attached to the end of the trough by tack welds which were subsequently incorporated in the butt weld. The intention was to start each weld approximately 100mm from the apex of the trough and weld vertically down, round the apex and up the other side without a break. This procedure was very difficult for the welder to follow. To make a vertical down weld a high welding current is required to prevent slag running ahead of the weld pool and becoming trapped within the weld as it solidifies. Vertical up welding on the other hand requires a low current to avoid undercut. Unfortunately the Series C specimens were made without the special welding equipment which allows the current to be changed during a weld pass and several showed evidence of remedial work at the apex of the trough. Even with this special welding equipment it was not possible to achieve acceptable productivity and defect rates with a large number of welders under site conditions, so this welding procedure is unlikely to be used in future.

As was to be expected, all the fatigue cracks initiated at the root of the splice weld but, rather surprisingly, most were in the weld on the web of the trough rather than at the more highly stressed apex. This was due to the fact that, in each of the joints, the residual stresses due to welding were compressive at the apex and tensile in the web. Indeed, it seems probable that the main reason for the differences in strength between the three series of butt welded specimens may well have been differences in the level of compressive residual stress.

Confirmation of the fact that the residual stress distribution was an important variable was

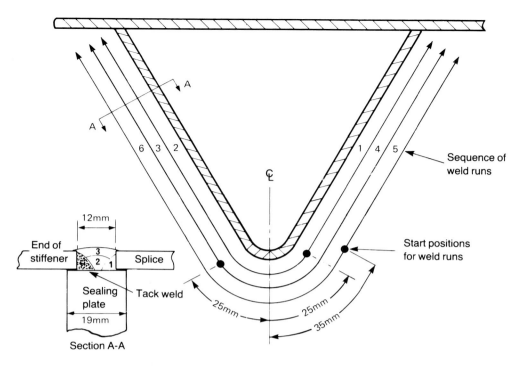

*Figure 10.4  Weld procedure for type A splice joint*

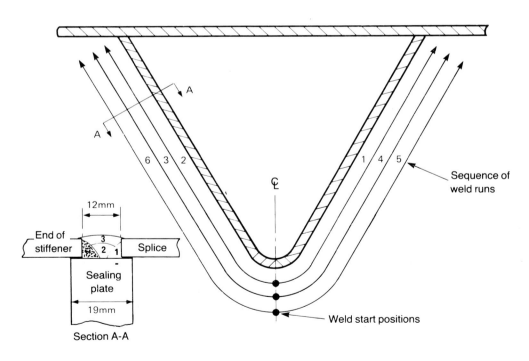

*Figure 10.5  Weld procedure for type B splice joint*

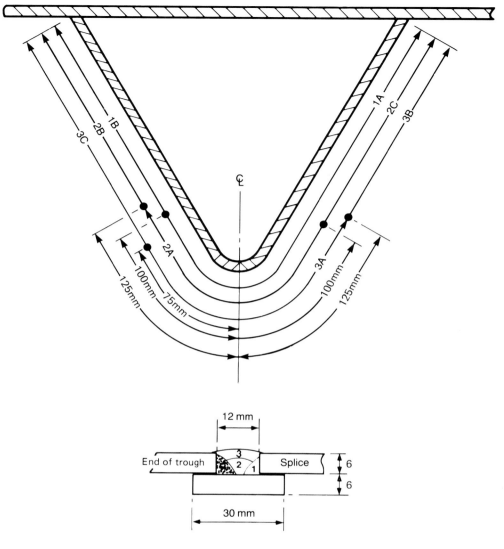

*Figure 10.6 Weld procedure for type C splice joint*

obtained by testing some of the Type B specimens after stress relief. It will be seen from Fig. 10.3 that this led to a significant increase in strength at long life and that the majority of the failures in those specimens were now located at the apex of the trough.

At first sight, the results shown in Fig. 10.3 suggest that the butt welded splice joint could be assumed to fall in BS 5400 Class C, for which the mean -2 standard deviations design stress at $2 \times 10^6$ cycles is 124N/mm2. However, such an assumption would rely heavily on the fact that compressive residual stresses would always be present at the trough apex. In fact, variations in welding procedure and repairs around the apex of the trough, which are likely to occur under site conditions, could lead to an unfavourable pattern of residual stresses and reduced fatigue performance.

In view of this possibility it is interesting to re-analyse the results in terms of the stress range at the point of crack initiation, which was assumed to correspond to the centre of length of the final crack. The results expressed in that form are shown in Fig. 10.7 and clearly they correspond to the fatigue strength which would be obtained from a welding procedure which led to tensile residual stress at the point of failure initiation. Indeed, also shown is a single result for a Type C weld, which had to be repaired at the apex of the trough and which subsequently failed at that point, obviously in the presence of tensile residual stresses induced by the repair weld. Clearly these results are now considerably lower than Class C and in fact it can be seen from Fig. 10.7 that Class D is more appropriate.

As far as the double lap fillet welded splices are concerned, the S-N curve shown in Fig. 10.3 is almost precisely coincident with the Class E mean curve. Indeed, the results are well above the mean -2 standard deviations curve for Class D but, in view of the relatively small number of results, Class E appears to be a more appropriate classification. It will be noted that this represents a considerable increase in strength compared to 'normal' transverse load-carrying fillet welded joints (Class F2) which is only partly explained by the fact that the trough plate thickness was only 6mm. Nevertheless, the use of a thicker trough might well lead to a reduction in fatigue strength.

In the case of the single lap fillet welded splices it is not possible to derive an accurate classification for toe failure since, as noted previously, all cracks were through the throat of the 8mm fillet welds. However, the weld toe strength was at least equivalent to Class G (66N/mm2 mean strength at 2 x 10⁶ cycles). Meanwhile, the nominal weld throat shear stress was approximately equal to 1.12 times the stress in the trough, or about 72N/mm2 at 2 x 10⁶ cycles. This is far above the stress quoted for Class W (56N/mm2 mean stress). Thus it seems reasonable to treat this type of joint as being in Class G for the stress in the trough and Class W for the stress in the weld; nevertheless, it is not a type of joint which can be recommended.

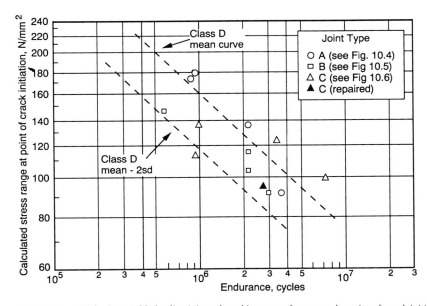

*Figure 10.7  Test results for butt welded splice joints plotted in terms of stress at the point of crack initiation.*

137

# 11 BUTT JOINTS IN THE DECK PLATE

It is usually most practical to make the butt welds in the deck plate of orthotropic decks from one side only. Under transverse repeated loading the fatigue strengths of such joints are usually critically dependent on the root condition so that, to ensure that full root penetration is achieved, and that the welds are free from significant defects and that they have good alignment, it is common practice to make the weld on to a permanent backing bar. This also assists site assembly, particularly if fit-up is poor. Often, the backing strips are tack welded to one or both of the plates to be joined.

In butt welds on permanent backing bars which are transverse to the direction of stress there are three possible sites for fatigue cracking, as shown in Fig. 11.1(a). They are:

1) From the toe of the butt weld, for which the fatigue strength would be expected to be much the same as that of a butt weld made from both sides by the same process;
2) From the weld root through the weld metal, which is the most usual mode of failure;
3) If the backing bar is tack welded in position, from the toe of the tack (fillet) weld.

When the joint is parallel to the direction of stress, however, the mode of failure, and the fatigue strength, is more usually dictated by the presence of the tack welds attaching the backing bar to the plate. In that situation each end of each fillet weld forms a stress concentration from which the fatigue cracks initiate (Fig. 11.1(b)).

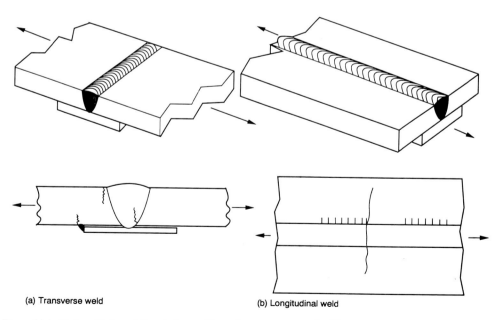

(a) Transverse weld      (b) Longitudinal weld

*Figure 11.1  Modes of fatigue failure in butt welds made on a permanent backing*

138

At the time of the construction of the Severn and Forth Bridges there were very few fatigue test data for butt welds on backing bars, and those that did exist were remarkably scattered. Much of the work that was carried out was therefore aimed at the generation of basic design data, but it included brief studies of the influence of various subsidiary variables such as plate thickness, mean stress and residual stresses.

## 11.1 Longitudinal butt welds, axial loading

If a butt weld is made on a backing bar which is not tack welded in position using fillet welds, or if the fillet weld is continuous, longitudinal welds would be expected to have relatively high fatigue strengths. Under such circumstances fatigue cracking would be likely to initiate from stop/start positions in manual welds, weld ripples in automatic welds or buried defects in both types and the joint would be classified as C for automatic welds and D for manual welds.

However, as noted previously, if the backing bar is tack welded in position with short lengths of fillet weld, stress concentrations are introduced at the ends of the fillet welds, both in the plate and the backing bar, and fatigue cracking would be expected to occur in that region, as shown in Fig. 11.1(b). In order to check that expectation fatigue tests were carried out on two series of specimens (Fig. 11.2), one having the tack welds made in the downhand position and one with them made overhead.

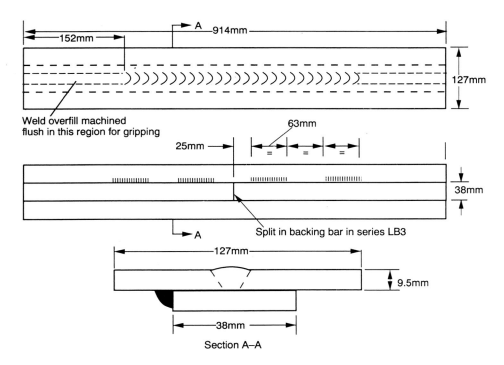

*Figure 11.2  Details of specimens with continuous longitudinal butt welds made on a permanent backing bar*

139

K

The results obtained are summarised in Fig. 11.3, from which it will be seen that there was not a large difference between the strengths of the two series, although the specimens with the tack welds made downhand clearly gave the higher strength. The difference can obviously be ascribed to the somewhat better end shape, and hence the lower stress concentration, of the downhand welds. As can be seen from Fig. 11.4, the primary mode of failure involved crack initiation in the backing strip followed by propagation via the longitudinal butt weld into the main plates. Meanwhile a subsidiary crack initiated from the end of the tack weld and propagated directly into the main plate. This behaviour is consistent with the fact that welds on a plate edge (in this case the edge of the backing bar) tend to give a lower strength than similar welds made on a plate surface.

Another feature of this type of joint which can influence the strength is the method of forming the backing strip. It used to be common, particularly in the case of long welds, for permanent backing strips to be formed from several individual lengths of strip, these merely being placed end to end to form the requisite length. The individual lengths of strip were not normally butt welded together. Since it was thought that this discontinuity might well cause a reduction in fatigue strength one series of tests was carried out to examine that possibility (see Fig. 11.2).

The results which were obtained are also shown in Fig. 11.3, from which it is obvious that the resulting fatigue strength was indeed very low, lower in fact than any 'standard' form of welded joint. At 2 x 10⁶ cycles the mean strength, based upon the gross cross-sectional area (including the backing strip), was only about 51 N/mm2. As was expected, all the failures were initiated at

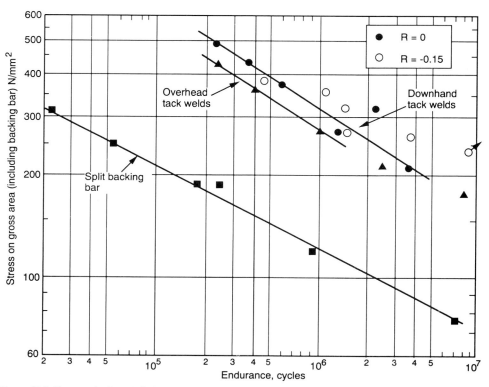

*Figure 11.3  Test results for axially loaded longitudinal butt welds on a permanent backing bar (R=0)*

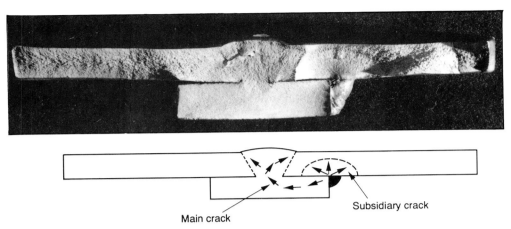

Figure 11.4 *Typical fracture surface of longitudinal butt weld made on a continuous backing bar.*

the discontinuity rather than at the ends of one of the tack welds. Examination of the fracture surfaces showed that, in fact, all the welds had hot cracks at the weld root which must have existed prior to the fatigue testing. By varying the gap between the two adjacent pieces of backing strip, several attempts were made to obtain specimens without hot cracking, but this was found to be impossible. It therefore seems likely that similar cracking will exist in such joints made in service, and that the results are typical.

It is worth noting that this type of detail is not covered by many fatigue design Standards but that, in view of the low strength associated with it, it should not be used. Under fatigue conditions discontinuous backing bars should be avoided and, if they are used, they should be butt welded together to eliminate the 'crack'.

## 11.2 Transverse butt welds, axial loading

In the context of transverse welds, the investigation was concerned with several geometric variations (Fig. 11.5). They included, in particular:

a)   the influence of plate thickness, which was studied by testing joints of Type A (Fig. 11.5) in both 12.7 and 25mm thick plates;

b)   the influence of a 2mm gap between the main plate and the backing strip, again using joints of Type A;

c)   a comparison of the strengths of joints made with the backing strip fillet welded either to one or to both plates or with no fillet welds (Specimen Types A, B and C).

In addition, a study was carried out of the influence of residual stresses. Since it is not easy to measure residual stresses at the weld root under a backing bar, which is where fatigue cracking normally initiates, it was considered that the best way to explore their influence was to make comparative tests on as-welded and stress relieved specimens of Type A, taking care to employ large enough specimens to contain residual stresses comparable with those expected to be present in real structures. To provide further information on the effect of high tensile residual stresses,

141

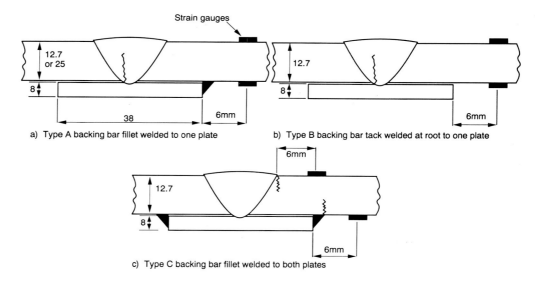

a) Type A backing bar fillet welded to one plate

b) Type B backing bar tack welded at root to one plate

c) Type C backing bar fillet welded to both plates

*Figure 11.5  Details of transverse butt welds included in the test programme*

and regarding them as being effectively equivalent to dead-load applied stresses, stress relieved specimens were also tested under conditions of high tensile mean stress for comparison with similar tests at R = 0.

In view of the fact that it was found that residual stresses played a particularly important role in the fatigue behaviour of this type of joint, it is convenient to start by considering that part of the work.

## 11.3  Influence of residual stresses

It is generally assumed that in as-welded joints the residual stresses in the region where fatigue cracks initiate are tensile and therefore that they may have a detrimental effect on fatigue life, depending on the nature of the applied loading (2). As a consequence, fatigue design rules (e.g. BS 5400 Part 10) are based on stress range regardless of applied mean stress to allow for the presence of high tensile residual stresses.

In view of this, the test results obtained for 12.7mm thick joints in the as-welded and stress relieved conditions respectively (Fig. 11.6) were rather surprising. Although the results are fairly scattered it is still possible to see that, with one exception, stress relief reduced fatigue strength. The implication of this finding was that the residual stresses in the weld root region of the as-welded joints, acting in the direction of fatigue loading, were compressive, not tensile. This was checked by measuring them in two as-welded specimens and it was found that in both instances the residual stress at the weld root was indeed compressive with values of 36 and 75N/mm2.

The presence of compressive residual stresses will have the effect of reducing that part of the applied stress which is effective in propagating a fatigue crack. Thus, in the present case it is not surprising that stress relief of the joints led to a reduction in fatigue life. In contrast, the application of part compressive fatigue loading onto a compressive residual stress field would

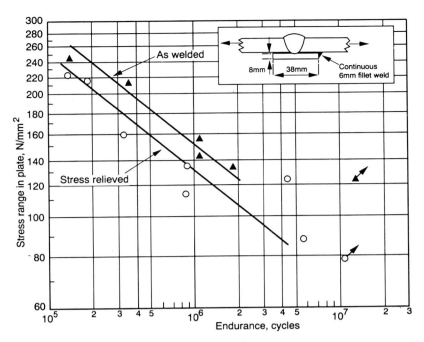

Figure 11.6 Comparison of test results for as-welded and stress relieved joints, 12.7mm thick

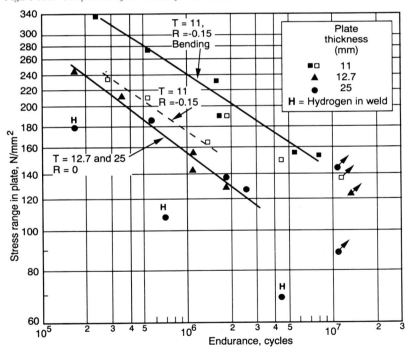

Figure 11.7 Test results for as-welded transverse butt welds, R≈0

result in an increase in fatigue life. This seems the likely explanation for the fact that test results obtained from 11mm thick joints tested at R = 0.15 were relatively high compared to the results for R = 0 (Fig. 11.7).

143

In fact it was found, by measurement, that there was quite a wide variation in the magnitude of the residual stresses, not only between test series but also between individual specimens in the same series. This may well be part of the explanation for why the test results in the literature for this type of joint tend to be very scattered. It seems clear, however, that although the tests outlined above showed the specimens to contain residual compressive stresses at the root, they could, in practice, be tensile (due, for example, to crossing welds) and it would therefore be unwise to assume that beneficial residual stresses would necessarily always be present.

It was in the light of this situation that the remainder of the investigation was carried out using stress relieved specimens.

## 11.4  Influence of mean stress

The main objective in studying the influence of tensile mean stress was, in fact, to provide further information on the effect of high tensile residual stresses since, as noted above, there was no way of guaranteeing that such stresses would not sometimes exist at the weld root. To this end two series were tested with tensile mean stress, one corresponding to the minimum specified yield stress of the steel (355 N/mm2) and the other to half that value.

A comparison of the results with those obtained at R = 0 is shown in Fig. 11.8. From this it can be seen that a mean stress equal to half yield stress only had a small effect on fatigue strength, although there did appear to be a significant reduction in strength when the mean stress was equal to the nominal yield stress. On the other hand the validity of those results is questionable since all the specimens did yield.

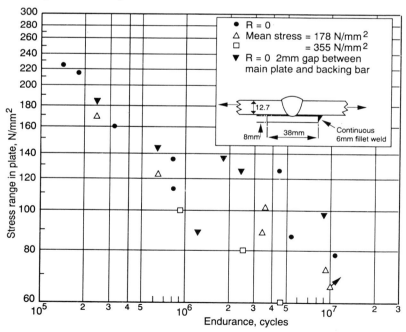

Figure 11.8  Test results for axially loaded stress relieved transverse butt welds, 12.7mm thick

144

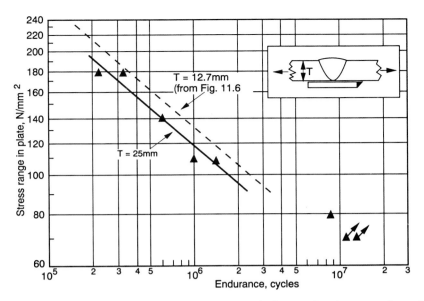

*Figure 11.9 Influence of plate thickness on the fatigue strength of stress relieved transverse butt welds (R=0).*

## 11.5 Influence of joint geometry

Since transverse butt welds on a permanent backing bar involve the formation of a stress concentration transverse to the direction of stress, it seems reasonable to expect that, like transverse non-load-carrying fillet welds, fatigue strength should decrease with increasing thickness. In order to check this expectation fatigue tests were carried out on stress relieved joints of Type A of both 12.7 and 25mm thickness. The results (Fig. 11.9) do indeed show a small reduction in strength with increasing thickness.

The second geometrical variable to be studied was the influence of a 2mm gap between the backing bar and the plates. The influence of this variable can be seen in Fig. 11.8 which shows the results for two series, one with and one without a gap, tested at R = 0 in the stress relieved condition. The objective was to determine the importance of fit-up in the joint and, as will be seen in Fig. 11.8, although the results are scattered they seem to be in reasonable agreement. Thus, the poor fit-up did not reduce the fatigue strength of the joint. From a practical viewpoint this suggested that the fatigue strength of this type of joint is very tolerant to poor fit-up, provided that penetration of the butt weld to the backing bar is achieved.

With regard to the method of attaching the backing strip, a summary of the results which were obtained is shown in Fig. 11.10. From this it is clear that the joints with the backing bar fillet welded to both plates tended to give relatively high strengths. This was rather surprising since, normally, fillet welded attachments to stressed plates which fail by fatigue crack growth from the weld toe have fatigue strengths similar to or lower than butt welds made on backing bars. However, the finding is compatible with the fact that the joints having the backing bar attached by a single fillet weld invariably failed in the butt weld from the root. This implies that, with this type of joint, the butt weld root has a more severe stress concentration than the fillet weld toe, but that, with the backing strip fillet welded across the root it was to some extent 'protected'. In

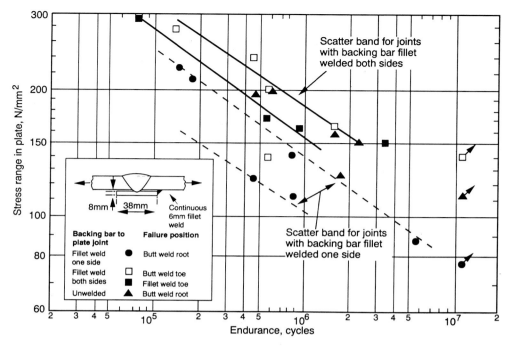

*Figure 11.10    Influence of the method of attaching the backing bar on the fatigue strength of stress relieved transverse butt welds (R=0)*

practice, however, having the backing strip fillet welded to both plates when making long welds tends to cause defects in the butt weld resulting from the gas trapped under the backing strip. In any case, if access is available to both sections of the joint to make the fillet welds, it would normally be preferable to omit the backing strip completely and make the joint as a butt weld from both sides.

An alternative method of holding the backing strip in place is to tack weld it to one of the plates at the weld root, the tack welds subsequently being remelted and buried in the butt weld. As can be seen from Fig. 11.10 this also gave a relatively high fatigue strength, even though failure initiated at the weld root and propagated through the butt weld.

## 11.6  Transverse butt welds in bending

In the course of the work only one series was tested in bending and that was at R = -0.15. A direct comparison between those results and some results for a similar series tested at the same stress ratio under axial loading is shown in Fig. 11.7. Although the scatter in the results for the axially loaded specimens was considerable, it will be seen that the specimens tested in bending clearly gave the higher strength, typically by about 20%.

146

## 11.7 Joint classification

It will have been noted that the great majority of the fatigue tests referred to in this chapter were carried out under axial loading rather than bending. To some extent, therefore, the strengths which were obtained are probably unrealistically low in the context of orthotropic decks, where the primary loading mode of the deck plate will be bending. Equally it is not surprising that the results, in general, confirm the classification contained in BS 5400, Part 10, which were also based upon results for axially loaded specimens. These are:

a)  Longitudinal welds, failing from tack welds between the backing bar and the plate (see Fig. 11.3) Class E
b)  Transverse welds, failing from the weld rootClass F

The single S-N curve (Fig. 11.7) for transverse welds in bending suggests that the fatigue strength is very much higher under that mode of loading, but more test results are required before that can really be confirmed.

Finally, there should be a complete ban on the use of discontinuous backing bars, and it seems unattractive to make transverse joints with the backing bar fillet welded to both plates being joined.

L

# 12 FATIGUE ASSESSMENT

As has been noted previously, the fatigue design rules in current Standards are not really relevant to the design of orthotropic decks. Indeed, in BS 5400 (Part 10) it is specifically stated that the stress analysis and classification of details in such decks are complex and beyond the scope of the Standard. This comment arose from the fact that, at the time of the last revision of the Standard, insufficient research had been carried out either to define the fatigue strengths of the various joints, which typically occur in orthotropic decks, or to define the relevant stresses to be used in their design. However, in the light of the work summarised in the previous chapters, it seems reasonable to deduce that much more useful guidance can now be given, even if all the answers are not yet know.

One point which does seem to be clear, however, is that if the full benefit of using an orthotropic deck is to be obtained it is necessary to use the most rigorous fatigue design approach available; the simplified fatigue design methods permitted in BS 5400 are not suitable. This implies that it is necessary to know, in some detail:

1  The loading spectrum both in terms of its overall composition and its transverse distribution on the deck.
2  The relevant influence lines of stress for the various joints.
3  The effect of the surfacing on those stresses, including the influence of the surfacing temperature.
4  The relevant joint classifications.

In the course of the investigations outlined in this document, information has been obtained on each of these aspects of the problem.

As far as the stresses are concerned, it is certainly possible to use analytical methods to calculate stresses at welded connections due to traffic loading. However, their accuracy may be limited and this may be very significant in view of the fact that fatigue life is inversely proportional to at least the cube of the stress range. Consequently it was considered that experimental stress measurements would provide the simplest and most accurate basis for fatigue assessments.

Thus, stresses at each of the welded joints due to traffic loading were obtained from load tests, either on a full size deck panel in the laboratory under a single wheel load, or on an actual bridge using a test vehicle with known wheel loads. In both cases the load was applied at many different positions on the deck, and strains were measured by ERS gauges at each welded joint. Stress influence lines were calculated from the measured strains.

Given the simple stress influence lines it was possible, by assuming that stress is proportional to wheel load, to build up influence lines for the various vehicles in the assumed commercial vehicle loading spectrum, as defined in Table 11 of BS 5400, Part 10, 1980. Then, by superposition, a stress spectrum was calculated for each joint by performing a rainflow or reservoir count (see BS 5400, Appendix B) on each influence line, taking account of the assumed transverse distribution of vehicles (BS 5400, Fig. 17). For an existing structure the centreline of the transverse distribution of traffic can be determined by observation on the bridge, but clearly it is also possible to assess the effect of proposed changes to the position of traffic lanes.

The experimental approach also has the advantage that the stress reduction (and fatigue life enhancement) of the surfacing may also be considered. This effect is extremely difficult to model mathematically and as such 'this effect should only be taken into account on the evidence of special tests or specialist advice' (BS 5400, Part 10, clause 6.1.4.2). It will be shown later that if this effect is not taken into account, most connections close to the wheel tracks on existing bridges would fail to meet the required (in the UK) 120 year fatigue life.

In parallel with that work numerous fatigue tests were carried out (see Chapters 6-11) to define the constant amplitude S-N curves for the various joints that exist in orthotropic decks. One of the primary aims of those tests was to obtain sufficient results to enable each joint to be assigned to one of the standard weld classes defined in BS 5400, Part 10.

Fatigue lives were then calculated using the Palmgren Miner cumulative damage rule, the details on the Severn Crossing being used as a basis. The techniques and procedures can, however, be applied to any bridge deck of that type.

In fact, in the course of the investigation comparative calculations were carried out using three different methods of calculation dependent on the method used to obtain the stresses:-

(a)    Method 1 used the single wheel influence line data from the laboratory or bridge tests to determine the fatigue life for the unsurfaced deck.

(b)    Method 2 used a similar procedure to calculate lives from the data from the surfaced deck but went on to assess the overall life taking into account the flow of vehicles across the bridge at different temperatures throughout the year.

(c)    Method 3 made use of the data obtained directly from a bridge under actual traffic loading.


*(a) Method 1: Unsurfaced Deck - Static Test Data*
A computer program was developed to calculate fatigue lives from experimentally determined stress influence surface data and the loading of BS 5400 part 10. Data preparation mainly involved the entry of the single wheel stress data and the co-ordinates of the loading positions. Influence lines for the vehicle types described in Table 11 of BS 5400 were calculated by superposition of the single wheel data. The vehicle influence lines were calculated at a number of transverse positions across the deck and due allowance was made for the transverse distribution of vehicles defined in the 'multiple paths' clause (C.1.4) of BS 5400. For the assessment of existing structures, the centreline of the transverse distribution of traffic could obviously be determined by observation on the bridge.

A stress spectrum was calculated from the vehicle influence line data using the 'rainflow' cycle counting technique. Fatigue lives were calculated using appropriate S-N data and applying the Palmgren-Miner method of damage summation.

With this approach the program run time is short. It is therefore easy to repeat the calculations with traffic centred at a number of different transverse positions, to determine the effect of proposed changes to the position of traffic lanes on a bridge.

*(b) Method 2: Surfaced Deck - Dynamic Test Data*
Fatigue lives were calculated in a similar way from data obtained from load tests on the surfaced bridge. The data processing was more complex, since analogue-to-digital conversion of the strains recorded onto magnetic tape was required. It was also necessary to deal with the fact that the influence lines from the test vehicle were at random transverse positions.

Fatigue lives thus calculated necessarily relate to the surfacing temperature at the time of the load test. To determine an overall life, relating to conditions throughout the year, allowance must be made for the variation of temperature throughout the day and year and the variation in the flow of traffic at different times of the day. However, using the information on deck temperature as a function of time (see Chapter 5) and on the flow of HGV traffic, also as a function of time, it was possible to estimate the traffic flow at different temperatures. It was then possible to apportion the fatigue lives at specific temperatures to determine an overall value relating to the whole year.

*(c) Method 3: Surfaced Deck - Traffic Stress Data*
Stresses at twelve welded joints in the deck of the Wye Bridge were monitored for 13 months. Stress spectra were stored by the recording equipment at one hour intervals. Traffic flow was monitored during the recording period and the time and duration of interruptions to the flow over the instrumented area due, for example, to lane closures or traffic management schemes, was noted. Fatigue damage was calculated from the stress spectra for the total recording period, and factored to take account of interruptions to give an estimate of fatigue life for each joint.

A summary of the fatigue lives of six connections on the Wye Bridge, calculated using each of the three methods, is shown in Table 12.1. All lives relate to a 2.3% probability of failure (using mean -2 standard deviations S-N data) and a traffic flow of 800,000 HGVs per annum. This was the observed traffic flow and is less than the 1.5 million vehicles required by BS 5400. The centre

**TABLE 12.1     ESTIMATED FATIGUE LIVES FOR JOINTS ON THE WYE BRIDGE**

| Joint (weld class) | *Fatigue life of joint (years)* | | |
|---|---|---|---|
| | Unsurfaced | Surfaced deck | |
| | Method 1 | *Method 2* | *Method 3* |
| | static test | *Dynamic test* | *Traffic stress* |
| Trough to deck (F) | 6.5 | 94 | >120 |
| Longitudinal butt weld (F) | 5.9 | >120[1] | >120 |
| Web of box to deck (D) | 41 | >120 | 40[2] |
| Trough to cross-beam (G) | 4.3 | 13 | 18 |
| Cross-beam to deck (D) | 94 | >120 | >120 |
| Transverse butt weld (F) | 35 | >120[1] | >120 |

Notes:
1     Insufficient data for full assessment but expected value >120 years
2     Surfacing cracked over web

of the transverse distribution of traffic was assumed (in methods 1 and 2) to be at the centreline of the carriageway. Where appropriate, surfaced lives relate to the hand laid mastic experimental surfacing. The assumed weld classes are shown in brackets. The lives given in Table 12.1 do not take account of damage sustained prior to resurfacing, but would apply to repaired joints or to similar connections on a new bridge. It can be seen that, for the unsurfaced deck, none of the details met the 120 year design life required by the code.

Some of the assumptions in method 2 were chosen to give a conservative (low) estimate of fatigue life. For two of the connections the data obtained were at an insufficient range of temperatures to enable overall fatigue lives to be calculated. Nevertheless, the data suggest that both these joints would have fatigue lives in excess of 120 years on the surfaced deck, even though the calculated lives were low on the basis of the unsurfaced deck assumptions.

Data for the method 2 calculation were obtained within six months of resurfacing the strain gauged area. Collection of data for the method 3 calculation began 12 months after resurfacing, by which time a longitudinal crack had developed over the web of the box. This explains the loss of effectiveness of the surfacing for this connection and the fact that the estimated life was similar to that for the unsurfaced deck in this case.


## 12.1  The effect of surfacing

As discussed in Chapter 4, the bridge deck surfacing can lead to large reductions in stress in the steel deck, although the properties of the surfacing are very dependent on temperature. As can be seen from Table 12.1, for most connections the very short fatigue lives calculated for the unsurfaced deck are increased to above the 120 year design life by the surfacing. One exception is the trough to cross-beam connection where the stiffening effect of the surfacing has only a small influence on the stresses at the apex of the trough. Failures of this connection have occurred in service.

The results suggest that failure of the trough to deck plate connection should not occur within the lifetime of a bridge (strictly, there is a calculated 2.3% probability of failure within 94 years) surfaced with mastic asphalt on an epoxy waterproofing layer. It should be noted that this surfacing system is stiffer than that originally used on the Severn Crossing and this difference may account for the fact that cracks have occurred in this connection after less than 20 years in service.

The results also showed on that bridge that the effectiveness of the surfacing can be completely lost if cracks develop in the surfacing over the welded connection. On some bridges it is quite common for cracks to develop over the web of box within weeks of resurfacing. These are normally controlled by sawcutting the surfacing and sealing the joint with a flexible bituminous material. Cracks can also develop over other hard spots, such as the troughs and cross-beams, that is the very connections the surfacing should be helping. This partly explains the difficulty of incorporating a surfacing factor in the codes. The search continues for a surfacing material with high stiffness (preferably at high and low temperatures) and a long fatigue life at the cold/brittle and hot/high-strain extremes.

## 12.2  The effect of the transverse position of the traffic

As can be seen from many of the transverse influence lines described in Chapter 3, the effect of the wheel load on the stresses at a typical connection near the deck plate tends to be very localized. In other words, the calculated fatigue life is very sensitive to the transverse position of the traffic. By way of example, it was shown that the life of the web of box to deck plate connection on the Wye bridge could be increased from 12 years to 80 years (unsurfaced deck, weld class F) by moving the traffic lanes 300mm towards the centre of the bridge.

Consideration may be given at the design stage to the relative positions of the traffic lanes and connections such as the web of box to deck and the longitudinal deck plate butt welds. For more frequently occurring connections such as the trough to deck plate connection (300mm intervals on Wye), there is little scope for improvement by this method.

## 12.3  Joint classification

In BS 5400 (Part 10), as in many other fatigue design Standards worldwide, welded joints are, for convenience, divided into a number of different classes, each class having its own S-N curves for use in design calculations. The allocation of joints to classes and the derivation of the relevant S-N curves were based upon an analysis of results from relatively small laboratory specimens, typically 13mm thick, tested under axial tensile loading. However, in the analysis of the data an attempt was made to allow for the absence of high residual stresses resulting from the relatively small specimen size.

As noted previously, joints in orthotropic decks were not included in that classification system, although it would seem sensible that they should be. However, there are several reasons why the classification of a joint in a deck may differ from that of a similar joint already in the Standard. For example, the stress distribution in the deck joint may be more complex, contain a much greater component of bending stress and have higher stress gradients around the joints. In addition some of the individual components of the deck (e.g. the longitudinal stiffeners) are usually significantly thinner than 'standard' fatigue test specimens, and thickness can influence fatigue strength.

In the earlier chapters an attempt has been made to outline the various fatigue tests which have been carried out on each type of joint and to compare the results with the design S-N curves in BS 5400. A summary of the recommended joint classifications emanating from those comparisons is set out in Table 12.2. Although these should apply to deck panels of similar geometry and plate thickness to those tested, care should be taken in applying them to designs which differ markedly from the test specimens. It should be borne in mind that the weld class depends on how the stress is defined. In general the classifications in Table 12.2 relate to the stress at right angles to the weld and 15mm from the weld root but that is not always the case; the notes in the table indicate the stress that is relevant.

For many of the joints it will be seen that the proposed classification is higher than that for comparable joints in BS 5400. This is consistent with the evidence that the fatigue strength of

**TABLE 12.2    SUGGESTED JOINT CLASSIFICATIONS**

| Joint and detail | Potential mode of failure | Suggested joint class | Relevant stress |
|---|---|---|---|
| Trough to cross-beam, fitted troughs 6mm thick: | | | |
| with 6mm fillet welds | In the weld throat | G | Stress in trough soffit |
| with 9mm fillet welds | | F | |
| with partial penetration welds | | F | |
| Trough to cross-beam, through troughs 6mm thick: | | | |
| Trough welded all round | from weld toe in trough | E | Stress range in trough apex |
| Welded on trough web, weld kept well clear of apex adjacent to weld end | From weld toe in trough web | D | Stress range in trough |
| Cope hole around trough to deck weld | In trough web from upper end of weld (in the cope hole) | G | |
| Ditto with welds meeting (no cope hole) | | F | |
| Longitudinal trough to deck joint made with fillet or partial penetration welds | (a) From weld toe in deck | D | 15mm from weld root in deck |
| | (b) From weld toe in trough | D | 15mm from weld root in trough |
| | (c) In weld throat | D[1] | Nominal weld throat stress calculated using equation 8.9 |
| Deck to cross-beam and | From weld toe in deck | D | |
| Deck to longitudinal web | From weld toe in cross-beam or web | D | |
| Trough splice joints: | | | |
| Butt welded | | D | |
| Double lap fillet welded | | E | |
| Single lap fillet welded | | G | Stress in trough |
| | | W | Weld throat shear stress |
| Butt joints in deck plate made on backing bars | | | |
| Automatic longitudinal welds with bar tack welded to plate | In deck plate from ends of tack welds | E[2] | Nominal stress in backing plate adjacent to butt weld |
| Transverse welds | From weld root in weld metal | F[3] | |

Notes:

1 This implies that a full or partial penetration weld gives an improvement in strength.

2 Backing bars must be continuous.

3 Backing bar should not be fillet welded to both plates being joined.

welded joints in thin plate is higher under bending stress than under axial stress (BS 5400 is based on axial test data).

## 12.4  The influence of plate thickness

It was noted above that the proposed joint classifications were only relevant to decks of similar thickness to those which were tested and, in particular, that the fatigue strength of welded joints can be influenced by plate thickness.

It has, of course, been known for a long time that plate thickness was likely to be a relevant variable under bending stresses. This was due to the fact that the stress gradient through the thickness of a 'thin' specimen would be steeper, and therefore less damaging, than in a 'thick' specimen. However, it is only in the relatively recent past that many tests have been carried out on welded joints in plates in bending.

Similarly, it has also been known for a long time that the fatigue strength of notched (but unwelded) specimens subjected to axial loading is also dependent on size. However, it is only relatively recently that it became apparent that the fatigue strength of at least some types of welded joints is dependent on thickness. As a result, the first time that a thickness correction factor was introduced into fatigue design rules was with the publication of the Department of Energy Guidance Notes in 1984.

The way in which that correction factor was derived was to compare all the available results, which had been obtained for joints of more than one thickness tested in a single investigation, and then to plot those results in terms of relative fatigue strength, normalised to a thickness of 32mm. It was on the basis of those results (Fig. 12.1) that the form of the thickness correction was chosen to be:

$$S = S_B \left( \frac{t_B}{t} \right)^{0.25}$$

where      $S$      is the fatigue strength of the joint under consideration
             $t$      is its thickness
             $S_B$     is the fatigue strength of the joint using the basic S-N curve
             $t_B$     is the thickness corresponding to the basic S-N curve

For design purposes it was assumed that for tubular nodal joints $t_B = 32$mm but that for other types of joint $t_B = 22$mm. In passing it may be noted that this is consistent with the data which were actually used for tubular joints, but for other types of joint the chosen value of $t_B$ is very much an illogical approximation; most of the data for such joints were derived using 12.7mm thick specimens, or thereabouts.

As far as other British fatigue design rules are concerned (e.g. BS 5400, Part 10 - Bridges) a thickness correction factor has not yet been incorporated, although the Department of Transport have issued their own rule for use in connection with the design of highway bridges. It is similar to that in the Guidance Notes, but slightly more severe.

Before considering the available test results it is worth noting that this particular problem can also be approached theoretically using fracture mechanics, and in work of that type it has been shown that the thickness effect does indeed continue to smaller thicknesses than 22mm. However, expressing the variation in fatigue strength with plate thickness as;

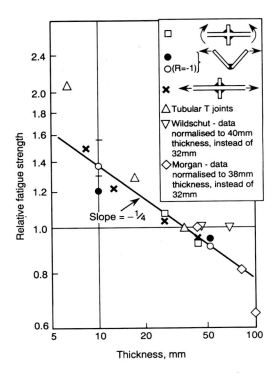

Figure 12.1
*Summary of results used in deriving the thickness correction factor in the Department of Energy Guidance Notes.*

$$\frac{S_1}{S_2} = \left(\frac{T_1}{T_2}\right)^r$$

where $s_1$ is the predicted fatigue strength for thickness $T_1$ and $s_2$ is the predicted strength for thickness $T_2$, it has been found that there tends to be a transition in slope (r) in the region 20-25mm. Thus, for transverse non-load-carrying fillet welds in bending, which is probably the most relevant mode of loading for joints in orthotropic decks, it has been shown by Gurney that the transition occurs at about 25mm, and that the relevant values of r depend upon the assumed crack shape. The values were:

|                      | T<25mm | T>25mm |
|----------------------|--------|--------|
| Continuous crack     | -0.11  | -0.14  |
| Semi-elliptic crack  | -0.19  | -0.22  |

It will be seen that all these values are less than the value 0.25 assumed in the Department of Energy Guidance.

Although the results for joints of different thickness tested in bending are not numerous, they are summarised in Fig. 12.2. Clearly there is a fair degree of scatter but nevertheless the existence of a thickness effect is obvious. In fact the best fit value of r was 0.15, which is well within the range of predictions set out above. For comparison Fig. 12.2 shows the corresponding design stresses relating to the Class F mean curve assuming $t_B = 13mm$ and $r = 0.25$.

155

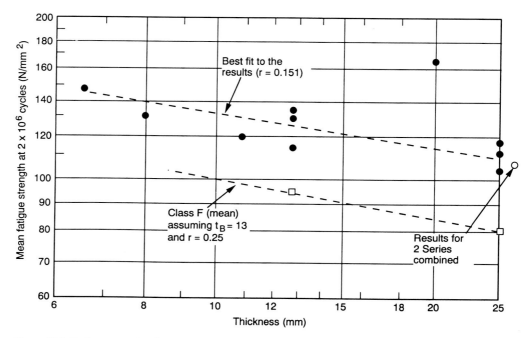

*Figure 12.2 Fatigue strengths of as-welded transverse non-load-carrying fillet welds in bending (at 2 x 10⁶ cycles)*

## 12.5 Detail design

As a result of the work a number of points relating to the detailed design of orthotropic decks have become apparent, and it may be helpful to summarise them here.

1.  For most joints the transverse influence line is short so that only joints directly under vehicle wheel tracks are at risk. Therefore wherever possible joints should be placed clear of the wheel tracks. Some joints, such as that between the longitudinal trough stiffener and the deck, which are repeated across the deck could be locally strengthened under the wheel tracks by specifying a larger fillet, or penetration weld. Alternatively, there is scope for considering the use of narrow troughs, with reduced spacing between them, in the region of the more heavily loaded wheel tracks.

2.  Some details, such as, for example, the cope hole in the cross-beam to permit passage of the trough to deck plate weld attaching troughs which pass through the cross-beam, are best avoided except on lightly trafficked bridges.

3.  Stresses in deck plate butt welds are higher than at most other welded joints. Particular attention should be paid to avoiding defects which reduce fatigue strength.

4.  For the same reason temporary attachments and 'construction details' on the deck plate should be avoided, or at least kept clear of the traffic wheel tracks.

5.  Although the joint classification relating to weld throat failure in trough stiffener to deck welds is D, based upon the stress in the weld throat calculated from equation 6 or 7 in

156

Chapter 8, that tends to disguise the fact that large improvements in strength can be obtained by increasing the weld size or, in particular, using full or partial penetration welds. This is a direct consequence of the form of equation [8.9] in Chapter 8, from which it follows that the stress in the weld is inversely proportional to $(l+p)2$, where $l$ is the weld leg length and $p$ is the amount of penetration. In terms of reducing the amount of weld metal that has to be deposited it is obviously more beneficial to increase the amount of penetration rather than the weld size.

# ACKNOWLEDGEMENTS

The impetus for the work described in this book derived primarily from the decision to build in Britain, after the Second World War, a number of long span steel bridges with orthotropic decks. Some of them, notably the Severn Bridge, were to be situated on major traffic arteries and subjected to very severe loading. At that time relatively little was known about just how severe that loading would be and even less about how the various types of joints inherent in such a design would behave under fatigue loading. There was, in fact, no relevant guidance in the Bridge Design Standard (BS 153) current at the time; indeed the same is still true today (1991). Suffice to say that it was obvious that there was a *potential* fatigue problem and the correctness of that suspicion was confirmed by the occurrence of some fatigue cracking in a trial deck panel, which had been inserted into a trunk road primarily to enable the stresses in the deck to be determined experimentally. In effect all the work summarised herein stemmed from that investigation.

I had the good fortune to be associated with the problem and to have the pleasure of working with Dudley Nunn, as a contractor, from the very early days. It must, however, be said that this book could never have been written without Dudley's assistance and access to his background knowledge. Particular thanks are due to him for his helpful and constructive criticism of the various drafts over many months.

In this respect I would also like to acknowledge and thank many other members of the TRRL staff, notably John Cuninghame, for their assistance in clarifying points of difficulty encountered in the drafting of the book. Without their assistance, too, the project could not have been accomplished.

Finally, I am indebted to my secretaries, Valerie Norden and, more recently, Rosemary Mortimer, for their patience and skill in converting my manuscript to something more readable.


Dr T R Gurney

# REFERENCES - List of published papers

BEALES, C (1990) Assessment of trough to crossbeam connections in orthotropic steel bridge decks. TRRL report RR 276.

BEALES, C and CUNINGHAME, J R (1990) Fatigue assessment of orthotropic steel bridge decks. Proceedings of conference on Bridge Management, Elsevier, London.

CUNINGHAME, J R (1982) Steel bridge decks: fatigue performance of joints between longitudinal stiffeners. TRRL report LR 1066.

CUNINGHAME, J R (1987) Strengthening fatigue prone details in a steel bridge deck. Proceedings of International conference on Fatigue of Welded Constructions, Brighton, The Welding Institute.

CUNINGHAME, J R (1990) Fatigue classification of welded joints in orthotropic steel bridge decks. TRRL report RR 259.

CUNINGHAME, J R and BEALES, C (1990) Fatigue crack locations in orthotropic steel decks. IABSE Proceedings P-150/90.

EMERSON, M (1973) The calculation of the distribution of temperature in bridges. TRRL report LR 561.

EMERSON, M (1976) Bridge temperatures estimated from the shade temperature. TRRL report LR 696.

EMERSON, M (1976) Extreme values of bridge temperatures for design purposes. TRRL report LR 744.

EMERSON, M (1977) Temperature differences in bridges: basis of design requirements. TRRL report LR 765.

HOLLIS, E and EVANS, R (1976) Motorway traffic patterns. TRRL report LR 705.

HOWELLS, H (1973) Temperature spectra recorded in surfacings on steel bridge decks. TRRL report LR 587.

JONES, M R (1977) Calculated deck temperatures for a steel box bridge. TRRL report LR 760.

LEONARD, D R (1972) A traffic loading and its use in the fatigue life assessment of highway bridges. TRRL report LR 252.

MADDOX, S J (1974) Fatigue of welded joints loaded in bending. TRRL report SR 84.

MADDOX, S J (1974) The fatigue behaviour of trapezoidal stiffener to deck plate welds in orthotropic bridge decks. TRRL report SR 96.

MORRIS, S A H and HOWELLS, H (1974) Derivation of stress spectra from measurements on orthotropic bridge decks during normal trafficking. TRRL report SR 44.

NUNN, D E and MORRIS, S A H (1974) Trials of experimental orthotropic bridge deck panels under traffic loading. TRRL report LR 627.

NUNN, D E (1974) An investigation into the fatigue of welds in an experimental orthotropic bridge deck panel. TRRL report LR 629.

NUNN, D E and CUNINGHAME, J R (1974) Stresses under wheel loading in steel orthotropic decks with trapezoidal stiffeners. TRRL report SR 53.

NUNN, D E and CUNINGHAME, J R (1974) Stresses under wheel loading in a steel orthotropic deck with V stiffeners. TRRL report SR 59.

PAGE, J (1980) Measurement of traffic loads and stresses in three steel bridges. TRRL report SR 597.

PAGE, J and TILLY, G P (1980) Some analyses of traffic data for three steel bridges. TRRL report SR 598.

SMITH, J W, CULLIMORE, M S G, FLEET, I D and LITTLE, C E (1985) Durability and stiffness of mastic asphalt on steel bridge deck plates loaded in Flexure. TRRL report CR 5.

STREAMS, B (1987) Prediction of future incidence of fatigue cracking from observed rates on a structure. Proceedings of International conference on Fatigue of Welded Constructions, Brighton, The Welding Institute.

TILLY, G P and PAGE, J (1980) A review of traffic loads and stresses in steel bridges. TRRL report SR 596.

Printed in the United Kingdom by HMSO at Edinburgh Press
Dd 294535 C8 9/92 (204086)